Down and Dirty

McFarland Classics

Anderson. *Science Fiction Films of the Seventies*
Archer. *Willis O'Brien*
Benson. *Vintage Science Fiction Films, 1896–1949*
Bernardoni. *The New Hollywood*
Broughton. *Producers on Producing*
Byrge & Miller. *The Screwball Comedy Films*
Chesher. *"The End": Closing Lines...*
Cline. *In the Nick of Time*
Cline. *Serials-ly Speaking*
Darby & Du Bois. *American Film Music*
Derry. *The Suspense Thriller*
Douglas. *The Early Days of Radio Broadcasting*
Drew. *D.W. Griffith's* Intolerance
Ellrod. *Hollywood Greats of the Golden Years*
Erickson. *Religious Radio and Television in the U.S., 1921–1991*
Erickson. *Syndicated Television*
Frasier. *Russ Meyer—The Life and Films*
Fury. *Kings of the Jungle*
Galbraith. *Motor City Marquees*
Harris. *Children's Live-Action Musical Films*
Harris. *Film and Television Composers*
Hayes. *The Republic Chapterplays*
Hayes. *3-D Movies*
Hayes. *Trick Cinematography*
Hill. *Raymond Burr*
Hogan. *Dark Romance*
Holland. *B Western Actors Encyclopedia*
Horner. *Bad at the Bijou*
Jarlett. *Robert Ryan*
Kinnard. *Horror in Silent Films*
Langman & Gold. *Comedy Quotes from the Movies*
Levine. *The 247 Best Movie Scenes in Film History*
McGee. *Beyond Ballyhoo*
McGee. *The Rock & Roll Movie Encyclopedia of the 1950s*
McGee. *Roger Corman*
McGhee. *John Wayne*
Mank. *Hollywood Cauldron: Thirteen Horror Films*
Martin. *The Allied Artists Checklist*
Nollen. *The Boys: ...Laurel and Hardy*
Nowlan. *Cinema Sequels and Remakes, 1903–1987*
Okuda. *The Monogram Checklist*
Okuda & Watz. *The Columbia Comedy Shorts*
Parish. *Prison Pictures from Hollywood*
Pitts. *Western Movies*
Quarles. *Down and Dirty: Hollywood's Exploitation Filmmakers*
Selby. *Dark City: The Film Noir*
Sigoloff. *The Films of the Seventies*
Slide. *Nitrate Won't Wait*
Smith. *Famous Hollywood Locations*
Sturcken. *Live Television*
Tropp. *Images of Fear*
Tuska. *The Vanishing Legion: ...Mascot Pictures*
Von Gunden. *Alec Guinness*
Von Gunden. *Flights of Fancy*
Warren. *Keep Watching the Skies!*
Watson. *Television Horror Movie Hosts*
Watz. *Wheeler & Woolsey*
Weaver. *Poverty Row HORRORS!*
Weaver. *Return of the B Science Fiction and Horror Heroes*
West. *Television Westerns*

Down and Dirty

Hollywood's Exploitation Filmmakers and Their Movies

by MIKE QUARLES

McFarland & Company, Inc., Publishers
Jefferson, North Carolina, and London

> The present work is a reprint of the library bound edition of
> Down and Dirty: Hollywood's Exploitation Filmmakers and
> Their Movies, first published in 1993. *McFarland Classics*
> is an imprint of McFarland & Company, Inc., Publishers,
> Jefferson, North Carolina, who also published the original
> edition.

Library of Congress Cataloguing-in-Publication Data

Quarles, Mike, 1957–
    Down and dirty : Hollywood's exploitation filmmakers and their movies / by Mike Quarles.
        p.   cm.
    Includes index.
    ISBN 978-0-7864-1142-9
    softcover : 50# alkaline paper ∞

    1. Motion picture producers and directors—United States.
    2. Sensationalism in motion pictures.   3. Sex in motion pictures.
    4. Violence in motion pictures.   5. Horror films—History and criticism   I. Title.
    PN1998.2.Q37   2001   791.43'023'0973—dc20   92-56683

British Library cataloguing data are available

©1993 Mike Quarles. All rights reserved

No part of this book may be reproduced or transmitted in any form or by any means, electronic or mechanical, including photocopying or recording, or by any information storage and retrieval system, without permission in writing from the publisher.

On the cover: A scene from Tobe Hooper's 1974 film *The Texas Chainsaw Massacre* (Courtesy Photofest)

Manufactured in the United States of America

McFarland & Company, Inc., Publishers
  Box 611, Jefferson, North Carolina 28640
    www.mcfarlandpub.com

to Frank and Leoma Quarles,
who will be mortified when they see this book

Acknowledgments

Mike Vraney found several rare ad mats of David Friedman's films and sent perfect copies to me.

Allan Greenfield gave me important information that helped locate several photographs.

Phil Vigeant trusted me with a collection of one-of-a-kind photos of Mark Pirro's career.

The staff at Jerry Ohlinger's quickly filled what must have seemed like a very strange order.

The chapters on Ted V. Mikels, Ray Dennis Steckler, and H. G. Lewis appeared in a somewhat different version in *Filmfax Magazine*.

Thanks to Ted Okuda for sending many rare ad mats from his collection.

Table of Contents

Acknowledgments	vii
Preface	xiii

1 • Ted V. Mikels, or How to Build a Corpse-Grinding Machine for $38   1

*Mikels uses whatever is at hand. For **The Corpse Grinders**, he took old lawnmower blades and used plywood to make a "corpse-grinding machine." His outlay was $38. This black-humored tale was in the can for $16,700 and hit number 11 on the national charts, mostly playing drive-ins.*

2 • Ray Dennis Steckler: Genre Filmmaking in a Funhouse Mirror   11

*After blowing his chances in Hollywood by almost running over Alfred Hitchcock with a movie paraphernalia "A frame" cart, Steckler brought a unique vision to his films, albeit one influenced by a lack of funds. His **Rat Pfink a Boo Boo**, a takeoff on Batman and Robin, was brought in for $8,000. The title was supposed to read "Rat Pfink and Boo Boo," but the guy doing the title cards goofed. When Steckler found out how much it would cost to fix, he let it go.*

3 • Humble Origins: Big-timers with Skeletons in Their Closets   23

*Francis Ford Coppola would have you believe his first was the horror film **Dementia 13**. Not so. Floating out there are two that came before it: **Tonight for Sure** and **Bellboy and the Playgirls**, both nudies. **Bellboy** even has segments in 3-D — this was Coppola's contribution. The bulk of the movie was imported footage of British burlesque queen June Wilkinson. Its distributors wanted to cash in on the flurry of 3-D films circa 1961.*

4 • H. G. Lewis: More Than Gore   29

*Lewis, who probably made more different kinds of movies than anybody else in this book, is known mainly for the genre he created: gore. While in Miami to shoot the nudie **Bell, Bare, and Beautiful**, he and his partner made the first gore film, **Blood Feast**. They took direct aim at the viewer's stomach; depictions of screen violence have never been the same. But what about those other movies? The ones without gore, mostly ignored?*

TABLE OF CONTENTS

5 • Russ Meyer: T and A and $ 41

His **The Immoral Mr. Teas** *was the first of the nudie-cuties, packing in audiences in theaters and courtrooms across America. Brushes with the law were of no consequence compared with the box office take, which set up Meyer as an independent producer-director. Noted film critic Roger Ebert wrote two of his films.*

6 • Kroger Babb: Who Was America's Foremost Hygiene Commentator?   51

In the 1930s and 1940s, when the Hays code kept a lid on what could be shown, a group of road agents sprang up to give audiences what they wanted: sin. Babb was the best of the roadshow men. His "birth of a baby" **Mom and Dad** *began with a sing-along of "The Star Spangled Banner," ended with color footage of a childbirth, and had an intermission lecture by "America's foremost hygiene commentator, Eliot Forbes." "Forbes" was whoever Babb could hire to hawk sex pamphlets.*

7 • John Waters: They Used to Call Him "The Prince of Puke"   57

His hit film **Hairspray** *shows just how far Waters has come. Look back at his first widely released film,* **Mondo Trasho**, *which started with a shot of chickens getting their heads chopped off. Waters won notoriety when he and his cast were arrested while trying to shoot the nude hitchhiker scene.* **Pink Flamingoes**, *the midnight movie that put both Waters and female impersonator Divine on the map, still brings in the crowds.*

8 • Trailers: Coming to This Theater   67

Previews of coming attractions are one of the most effective lures the exploitation filmmaker has. Often these little two- or three-minute "trailers" were better than the films themselves. Great collections of them are available on video, under names like **Sleazemania** *and* **Trasharama**: *everything from Ed D. Wood's* **Jailbait** *to softcore sleaze like* **The Smut Peddler**.

9 • George Romero: On Pittsburgh Zombies and an Italian Subgenre   71

Romero's gang struggled for years making commercials and training films, but the big money went to the New York agencies. So they decided to make a feature and put up $600 each. The movie: **Night of the Living Dead**. *It was followed by* **Dawn of the Dead** *(which would inspire an Italian subgenre, as American westerns had) and* **Day of the Dead**. *The spaghetti zombie film was born not from the hearts of Italian filmmakers, but from the heads of their bankers. Getting financing in the 1970s and 1980s meant copying other people's hits. The phenomenal success of* **Dawn of the Dead** *led to Lucio Fulci's* **Zombie** *and* **The Gates of Hell**, *among many others.*

10 • Fred Olen Ray: The Direct-to-Video King   79

Ray claims his first feature cost $298. The Florida television station he worked for let him borrow an old Auricon 16mm camera. There was some out-of-date black-and-white film stock in the cooler; not being sure if it was any good, the station gave it to him—and he made **The Brain Leeches**. *From these no-budget beginnings, he has gone on to make a fortune in the direct-to-video market.*

TABLE OF CONTENTS   xi

11 • Super 8: The New Medium of Choice   85

For years, exploitation filmmakers who couldn't afford 35mm shot in 16mm. Then, the Hunt brothers tried to corner the silver market. Silver salts, necessary to the production of film stock, went sky high. People were priced out of the medium. Some turned to video but these projects went nowhere. Audiences were accustomed to the "film look" and video looked second rate. Others began to experiment with Super 8 film: it was cheap, and the equipment could be had for a song. An Arong brothers Super 8 film about cockfighting in the Philippines, blown up to 35mm, outdrew Star Wars in the theaters it played. The direct-to-video release grew in importance. Mark Pirro shot A Polish Vampire in Burbank on Super 8 for $2,500. This video has grossed over $500,000 in tape sales and has been shown on the national cable network USA.

12 • Tobe Hooper: The Texas Chainsaw Massacre   99

Hooper made a documentary about Peter, Paul and Mary and the sensitive Eggshells, about the breakup of a commune. So how does such a fellow make a film like The Texas Chainsaw Massacre? He wanted to break through. He got the idea one Christmas: When shoppers elbowed him into the power tool section of a crowded store, nasty thoughts entered his mind. In an instant, he had the idea for his film. The movie he made has never been equaled in intensity, in mainstream film or otherwise. It caused a near riot at a sneak preview in San Francisco. The audience had first watched The Taking of Pelham One Two Three; it was followed by a film they would never forget.

13 • Dwain Esper: Exposing a Nation's Shame and Getting Away with It   111

Esper broke every article of the Hays code when it was at its strongest, in the 1930s. He showed drug use, sex scenes like the opening scenes from a stag film, and nudity. He got away with it by claiming that he was exposing these evils as a warning: Those who did such things would come to terrible ends. But they sure had a good time getting there.

14 • Andy Milligan: Period Dramas for Under $10,000   121

Milligan was an American who made many of his films in England for drive-ins. His first, Liz, came in under $7,000. He showed it to William Mishkin, who offered to take it if nudity was added. Milligan tacked on about 45 seconds' worth. Released as The Promiscuous Sex, the film had people lined up around the block. Milligan planned to rerelease all his films, keeping them going as long as possible, so he shot them as period pieces, to keep them from becoming dated. He used the same costumes in film after film.

15 • Larry Buchanan: Does Mars Need Women That Badly?   129

Filming Mars Needs Women, director Buchanan ran into a snag: not enough lights to shoot a scene. This didn't faze him; he shot it anyway, undercranking the camera so more light would get to the film. Undercranking, of course, would lead to other problems when the film was projected at normal speed. So, he had the cast move at half speed and say their lines v-e-r-y s-l-o-w-l-y. The result is one of the most bizarre sights imaginable. Buchanan would later make the docudrama Goodbye, Norma Jean.

16 • Doris Wishman: How Did a Nice Girl Like You Wind Up in a Book Like This?   139

The answer is, she was one of the top producers of nudist camp spectaculars, like **Nude on the Moon** *and* **Nature Girl***. She recruited some of the most notable talent on the burlesque circuit, getting Blaze Starr for* **Nature Girl** *and Chesty Morgan for* **Deadly Weapons***.*

17 • David Friedman: The Promoter   151

Friedman knew them all, from the old-time roadshow men, known as the Forty Thieves, to the Wizard of Gore, H. G. Lewis. He studied under the greatest exploitation huckster of them all, Kroger Babb, and went on the road with **Mom and Dad***, the most famous of the "birth of a baby" movies. His partnership with H. G. Lewis created such exploitation classics as* **Lucky Pierre** *and* **Blood Feast***.*

18 • Rogues' Gallery: A Cast of Dozens   175

Some people had one chance to make it in exploitation, but failed. Steven Hawkes worshipped H. G. Lewis years before it was fashionable. Hawkes's **Blood Freak** *gets a little of the attention it deserves. Stephen C. Apostoloff worked for years as producer-director, gaining little notice for himself, but making several profitable films. There are other "rogues."*

Index   187

Preface

Exploitation films are no different from any other kind of movie. All appeal to some desire or fear that the audience may have. Ony because they do it more directly, with perhaps a bit less finesse than a Hollywood product, are they branded as exploitation.

When a fellow has only $10,000 to make a film, and it's all *his* money that he's risking, who can blame him for opting to show "life in the raw," as the trailers used to claim? That such filmmakers could make any kind of film at all on the budgets they had was an achievement. That so many of their films are entertaining is a miracle.

This book is about those miracle makers—men like Fred Olen Ray, who made his first movie with a borrowed camera and out-of-date film stock, and hucksters like Kroger Babb, who would do anything to get people into the theaters. (Babb, when promoting his "birth of a baby" film *Mom and Dad*, hired vagrants to act as street-corner preachers. The vagrants would denounce the evil film, warning people to stay away from the theater. Then, they would pass out handbills stating the exact location of the theater to stay away from and the show times.)

It's about the taboo breakers and the trend setters, filmmakers like H. G. Lewis, whose landmark film *Blood Feast* would show screen violence as it had never been seen before. And the pioneers, like Dwain Esper, who would break the Hays code and get away with it. Esper's *Marihuana: Weed with Roots in Hell* would show drug use, and even nudity, in 1936, when the code was at its strongest.

Should exploitation films be taken seriously? Yes.

These films have broken ground that Hollywood would find fertile in later years. Although they seldom are launched for any cause so noble as fighting censorship, they do nonetheless exert such an influence. Someone shows something that Hollywood won't in order to make a dollar. Later, Hollywood takes it over, and it becomes mainstream.

Considered one way, these filmmakers are living the Horatio Alger version of the American dream. Many of them start with equipment that is little better than junk, with amateur casts, and with scripts they wrote on weekends. From these materials, they fashion a movie that people line up for blocks to see.

They are my heroes.

1

Ted V. Mikels, or How to Build a Corpse-Grinding Machine for $38

Smoke billowed from the wrecked auto. A man, knocked unconscious by the blow, sits slumped inside. When things seem their darkest, somehow they get darker. A madman with a yen for body parts comes along to collect a few for the creature he is building. The madman can be instantly recognized as John Carradine, mad scientist.

Then, here come the police and fire trucks, roaring up to save the day. But then, nobody had counted on the cops or the firemen showing up. It seems they hadn't been informed that a movie was being made.

No matter to Ted V. Mikels, director of *The Astro Zombies*. He just keeps the camera rolling and gets some great shots of fire trucks, police cars, and all kinds of commotion, for free. It looks great in the film. Very realistic.

"It was kind of delightful to see all those police cars pouring out of nowhere onto the property," says Mikels.

The Astro Zombies is one of several zero-budget gems made by Mikels. No matter how low the budget, Mikels always seems to get a lot of production value in every film. He does it by using anything and everything lying at hand. That, and a lot of ingenuity.

For instance, the wrecked-auto scene used an abandoned wreck that was on some land Mikels owned. The crew dressed it up just enough to use in the movie, put a smoke pot in it, and rolled the cameras. If it sounds cheap, what does it matter, as long as it looks good? As long as the illusion works.

Mikels knows a great deal about illusion. He started doing magic tricks at the age of five. As a teenager, he had his own show that he worked hard at to lengthen and improve. He became so good that he toured with the famous Mandrake. But a desire to create a different kind of magic took hold of him. Movie magic.

Poster art for *The Astro Zombies*, a zero-budget gem starring John Carradine and Tura Satana.

His entrance into the professional film world was as a stuntman. Here, an illusion helped him progress in his career. He was working on the movie *Indian Fighter*, starring Kirk Douglas and Alan Hale. The special effects men needed to shoot flaming arrows into wagons, but their phosphorous-tipped arrows didn't look real; rather than burning as they flew through the air, those arrows merely glowed.

Jack H. Harris Enterprises, Inc. presents **ASTRO ZOMBIES**

CAST

Holman	Wendell Corey
Dr. DeMarco	John Carradine
Eric Porter	Tom Pace
Janine Norwalk	Joan Patrick
Juan	Raphael Compos
Satanna	Tura Satanna
Franchot	William Bagdad
Tiros	Vince Barbi
Chuck Edwards	Joe Hoover
Dr. Petrovich	Victor Izay
Mike Webber	Wally Moon
Thompson	John Hopkins
Foreign Agent	Egon Sirany
Ginger	Lynnette Lantz
Chauffeur	Vic Lance
Lynn	Janis Saul
Astro Zombie	Rod Wilmoth

THE STAFF

Produced and Directed by	Ted V. Mikels
Screenplay by	Ted V. Mikels and Wayne M. Rogers
Photography	Bob Maxwell
Musical Score	Nick Carras

COLOR by DELUXE

Executive Producers ....Kenneth Altose and Wayne Rogers
A Ram Ltd. - T. V. Mikels Production

Note on this list of credits the screenplay writer and executive producer. It's Wayne Rogers, Trapper John on television's "M*A*S*H"!

Mikels showed them how to make arrows from pitch, the sap that oozes from pine trees, the way the Indians did. He used his own longbow to lob the flaming arrows you see in the film.

In the 1950s, Mikels worked for a time as a newsreel cameraman in Oregon. That job, and the stunt work, fit perfectly the kind of man he is. Mikels is a rugged, muscular man, who chose for his first feature project a rugged, outdoor action adventure entitled *Strike Me Deadly*.

In the movie, a young couple take summer jobs working for the U.S. Forestry Service. They look forward to a summer spent in a peaceful wilderness. Almost immediately, the idyll is broken. The man sees a murder take place. The killer pursues him through the woods, setting fires to destroy the evidence.

Mikels made the movie in 1960. It had loads of great action shots, some of which were stock footage Mikels shot himself. When you see an airplane fighting the flames, it's a real forest fire you're seeing.

Perhaps Mikels's only mistake was shooting the movie in black and white. Video distributors, who otherwise would be fighting for a chance at the film, have ignored it. "The minute you say 'black and white' you're shut off," says Mikels.

The initial expense of film stock left him with no choice but to use black and white. Mikels does hope to have the film colorized. Rather than seeing colorization as a negative force, he sees it as the only way to salvage his film, short of a complete remake.

Though not a big success, *Strike Me Deadly* did well enough to open doors for Mikels as a director and cinematographer. His work on several films finally led to his 1965 hit, *The Black Klansman*.

The rather unlikely story of a light-skinned black man who infiltrates the Ku Klux Klan to solve his daughter's murder, packed in the crowds. The film, also known as *I Crossed the Color Line*, is now regarded by most Mikels fans as a curiosity. Finally available on video, *The Black Klansman* is a prime example of topical subject (the civil rights movement) exploitation filmmaking of the kind television would take over in the 1970s and 1980s. It's also one of the first blaxploitation films. The movie made Mikels enough money to get into film distribution. This development marks the beginning of the best-known work by Mikels.

The Astro Zombies, mentioned at the beginning of this chapter, was made for peanuts and did great at the box office. Yet an even lower-budget film of his has proved to be his biggest grosser, *The Corpse Grinders*.

Following his basic rule of using whatever was lying at hand, Mikels built his corpse-grinding machine for the grand total of $38. He used some old plywood for the outside and some discarded lawn mower blades for "grinders." Red light bulbs costing 39 cents each were one of the few things he actually bought new for the machine.

On the whole, *The Corpse Grinders* is a delightfully cheap film. Mikels's economy went far beyond his corpse-grinding machine. The doctor's lab, a major set in the movie, looks suspiciously like somebody's kitchen. The grinder itself seems to be stationed in somebody's basement, though it is supposed to be part of a factory.

So how does Mikels manage to pull off his story, despite these handicaps? The answer is in his approach. He knew from the beginning that he couldn't aim for the viewer's jugular. To go at it in a deadly serious manner would simply have pointed out the project's shortcomings. So, Mikels decided to try to have a little fun with it, while still serving up some ghoulish scares.

The basic premise is this: Human flesh is the secret ingredient in a phenomenally successful brand of cat food. The problem for the manufacturer, Landau, is supply.

At first, Landau's solution is Caleb, a grave-robbing behemoth of a

This doctor's lab in *The Corpse Grinders* looks a lot like somebody's kitchen.

man, who seems to be a sort of sexton of the local cemetery. While Caleb robs the graves, Cleo, his wife, carries a doll about, which she cares for as if it were her child. (Neither supports the local mental health group.)

Caleb sells his corpses to Landau by the pound. "This one's a hundred and forty, that one over there is one forty, and this one over here is one seventy," he says, when they come to buy. But Landau is a scoundrel among scoundrels. He hasn't paid Caleb in ages, letting his bill with the body snatcher run up to well over $2,000.

Caleb says, "Next time, no money, no meat!" Landau gets a fiendish look in his eye. "Next trip, you'll get everything you deserve."

As if this sort of business wasn't enough to delight the fans of exploitation camp, Mikels throws another angle into the story. Not only do cats like the food, the taste of human flesh awakens a primal urge to dine on living humans. When the heroine of the story, a shapely blonde nurse, feeds her cat a can of Lotus brand cat food, the cat promptly attacks the doctor's neck. When other cat owners are attacked by their pets, the doctor and nurse decide to investigate.

And not a minute too soon. Landau and his henchman, Maltbie, have run low again on "raw material." Among their employees is a fearful, emaciated-looking fellow named Eddie. Eddie yearns to know what goes on in the back room, where the grinder is, but has always been too afraid to look. Landau becomes the soul of kindness, offering to show Eddie himself. Soon, Eddie falls to the demands of production, exiting as a case of Lotus. Landau decides that murder is the best way to maintain a steady supply of flesh for the grinder.

Caleb calls Landau, saying "I've got another boarder over here at my hotel, and we're just about full up." Which meant that his back room was filled with corpses.

Landau decides that Caleb's grave robbing is too dangerous and is apt to get them all caught (as if butchering employees, winos, and other unfortunates was a safe procedure). Landau does in Caleb; then, to prove how sadistic he is, he shoots Cleo and buries her alive.

Needless to say, a lot of folks get turned into Lotus cat food, and, of course, the snoopy nurse gets strapped to the conveyor belt by the leering Maltbie. It's altogether as much fun as you could ask for from a drive-in special.

Mikels has always been known for teaching newcomers the business, and on this film he had a full class. Virtually the entire cast and crew had either no experience or very little. The cameraman had shot some 16mm, but had never done anything in 35mm. On the first day, he was heard to shout to Mikels, "Ted, will you come over here and show me how to load this camera?"

Why would Mikels cut so many corners? Because he had only $1,700 to start *The Corpse Grinders*. He completed the film for $16,700. Lab costs and deferred payments put the final cost at $47,000.

This little film, running on a double bill with *The Undertaker and His Pals*, made it as high as Number 11 on national box office charts and had a long life on the drive-in circuit. It made back so many times its own cost that no one will say exactly how much it has made. Out on video, it still continues to turn profits.

The second half of the double bill, *The Undertaker and His Pals*, has often been thought to have been made by Mikels. This is a mistake. Mikels bought the film from others simply to have a double feature to distribute. In its original version it was extremely bloody, the filmmakers having decided to juice up their film with footage from surgical training films. Mikels had to edit out most of this material to make it playable. It left him with a film only 60 minutes long, the shortest film he has ever distributed.

For several years, Mikels lived in a house called Sparr Castle that actually was a castle. Mikels used it as the location for *Blood Orgy of the She Devils*, building a dungeon inside it for use in key scenes. Again, Mikels used resources at hand to craft the film.

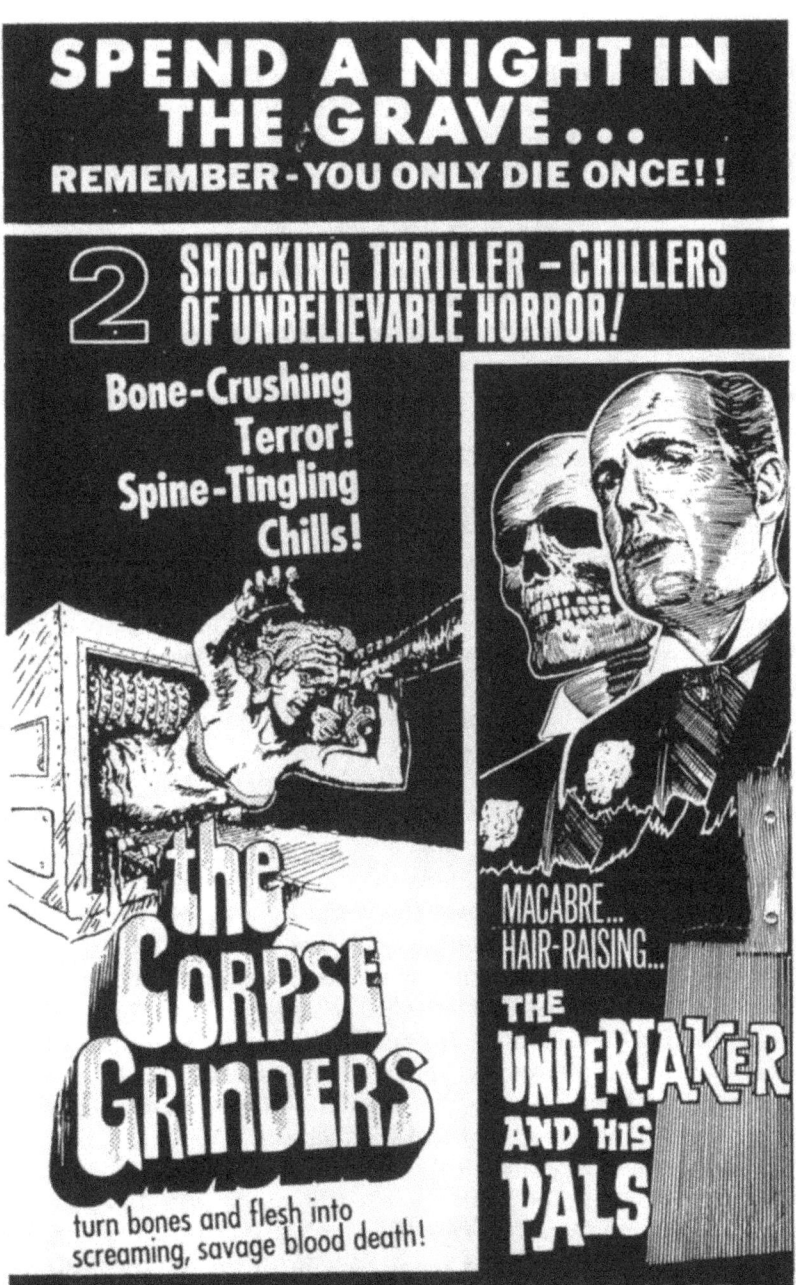

Mikels's box office–breaking double bill: *The Corpse Grinders* and *The Undertaker and His Pals*.

Ridiculous as it seems, Mikels had trouble advertising the movie. Some newspapers in 1973 wouldn't print movie titles with the word *blood* in them. Some refused the ads outright, others left out the word *blood*, and a few used the title *She Devils*.

Mikels has shown much of his own life and character in his films. His love of the outdoors can be seen in *Strike Me Deadly*. His sense of humor comes through in *The Corpse Grinders*. His own home of many years can be seen in *Blood Orgy of the She Devils*. But in no movie are the parallels as great as in *Alex Joseph and His Wives*.

This pioneering docudrama (a.k.a. *Obadiah 18*) is about a real man named Alex Joseph, who claimed ten wives — at the same time, under the same roof. The parts were acted by the actual people involved, recreating true events.

Where is the parallel? Mikels has had as many as ten women living with him at the same time. Mikels refers to them as "Castle Ladies."

The "Castle Ladies" came about because of the need to have everybody together when making a film. Valuable time could be lost because someone's car broke down or someone didn't know the way to a location. These ladies stay with Mikels, each of them working in some aspect of film production. As some leave, others come to take their place and learn about filmmaking from Mikels.

With or without Castle Ladies, Mikels has approximately 100 picture credits in various capacities, over 30 of them on features. His films have grossed over $100 million, yet he has received only a tiny fraction of the money, mostly because of the chicanery of distributors and theater chains.

More than money can be stolen from you in Hollywood. Ideas are precious, too. Say you have an idea about a group of beautiful female intelligence agents who go all over the world righting wrongs. Say one of them is named Sabrina. Say they are led by a guy named Charlie, who they talk to over a kind of globe-spanning walkie-talkie. You'd say you had the framework of the television show "Charlie's Angels," wouldn't you?

Yet this is a description of *The Doll Squad*, a movie Mikels made four years before "Charlie's Angels" appeared on television. It had a top-line cast, featuring Michael Ansara, Francine York, Rafael Campos, and Tura Satana, who had appeared in *The Astro Zombies*.

Despite experiences like the one with *The Doll Squad*, Mikels has continued to make films. The 1980s saw a trio of martial arts films by Mikels: *Devil's Gambit* and *Operation Overkill*, both starring Tiger Yang, and *Kill the Dragon*, which he produced, but did not direct. He returned to science fiction with *Space Angels* and put together the unusual hybrid film *Ten Violent Women*.

Ten Violent Women is the story of a gang of female jewel thieves, a likely subject for the action-loving Mikels. The women in the picture are tough, athletic, and generally good looking, but not classically beautiful. This seems to be a part of Mikels's philosophy of filmmaking. If a person is called on to dish out karate chops or shoot a gun, he or she had better be able to do it believably. Looks, for this type of picture, comes second.

This is a picture of varying styles that may fool the channel switcher who runs across it on cable television. At first, during the jewelry heist sequence, it has an almost lighthearted feel, like a pilot episode of a television show. But when the gang is caught and sent to prison, it takes a darker turn. The two parts are so different that it almost seems as if two movies were combined into one.

During the heist sequence, the women steal $1 million worth of jewels, including a priceless scarab that was owned by an Arab prince. This is a bad mistake because the Arabs immediately go after them.

The gang searches for a fence to unload the jewels on. They find none other than Ted V. Mikels himself, playing an oily thug who offers the women drugs in exchange for their jewels. The deal goes awry. Mikels's character is killed by the gang's leader, who stomps him to death with a pair of high heels.

The gang members grab the drugs and try to sell them. But the buyers turn out to be undercover cops, and the gang is headed for the jug. When the arrest is made, the gang's leader pulls a gun and is killed.

Now, two previously minor characters in the gang, Samantha and Becky, come to the forefront, and the film changes gears. For much of the rest of the picture, the viewer is treated to a fine example of a "women in cages" movie.

Naturally, there is a sadistic section boss, Miss Terry. The role is filled by Georgia Morgan, who gives the best performance of the film. She plays an iron-willed character who casts a lesbian eye toward Samantha, offering her special privileges if she cooperates.

Samantha is just as strong willed as is Miss Terry, and she refuses to comply. Miss Terry promises to make her regret it. The fireworks begin.

Miss Terry arranges for an ambush to take place in the showers. Here, the movie gets a little loony. The audience expects the standard nude shower sequence. Although the scene has a couple of naked extras, it seems that the lead actresses didn't want to do nude scenes, so they started taking showers with their underwear on.

Nevertheless, Miss Terry's pet inmates attack Samantha. Samantha and Becky whip them. Miss Terry is outraged. She tortures Samantha, while her assistant, a religious fanatic, kneels in the corner, praying for Samantha's soul.

After much more suffering, an elaborate escape is planned. Samantha's part in the plan is to act as if she has knuckled under to Miss Terry.

The two begin to make love. Then Samantha clobbers Miss Terry and steals her keys. Samantha, Becky, and their friends escape.

The movie shifts gears again, back to light television adventure material. Remember those Arabs? Well, they are still looking for their sacred scarab. In one of the most ridiculous coincidences on film, the women just happen to hitch a ride with one of the Arabs. They ask him to stop at a nightclub, where Samantha picks up the scarab she has hidden.

The Arabs entice the women into boarding a yacht, where they believe they can work their passage to the Mediterranean. It is the prince's yacht. He gets his scarab, and they get a free pleasure cruise to freedom. All's well that end's well.

Today, Mikels lives with his extended family in Las Vegas, having left his castle to go to the desert. Film backers asked him there, offering him money to make his movies if he relocated.

2

Ray Dennis Steckler: Genre Filmmaking in a Funhouse Mirror

One of the first jobs Ray Dennis Steckler had in Hollywood was on the "Alfred Hitchcock Presents" television show. He was a grip, one of the men responsible for moving equipment about on the set. It was a good job for a young man not long out of the army, and Steckler wanted to do his best at it. He would work hard and hustle.

One piece of equipment used on sets is known as an A frame. It has wheels and is used for carrying all sorts of loads. It would prove to be Steckler's undoing.

Steckler's task was to move an A frame down a long passageway. Time being money, the grips would grab their A frames and go flying off like banshees. Steckler took his and went tearing away, as fast as he could go.

Was it fate that placed Hitchcock himself just around the corner, directly in the way? It must have been a moment of frantic misery for Steckler when he rounded the curve. With the most athletic of efforts he dodged Hitchcock, missing tragedy only by inches.

Hitchcock gave him an evil glare, then whispered to an assistant who was standing nearby.

It was all plain enough for Steckler to figure out. "Don't say it, I'll go get my card," Steckler said. "I know."

Perhaps if things hadn't gone the way they did, Steckler would have stayed in the studio system, working his way up over the years. So mainstream's loss was exploitation's gain. Why? Steckler seems to have a unique vision of the world and of filmmaking—albeit a vision influenced by the lack of funds. His earliest directorial effort, *Wild Guitar*, was made for about $12,000. *Rat Pfink a Boo Boo*, the Batman and Robin takeoff, was brought in for only $8,000. That's less than the price of a coffee break on most Hollywood features.

People marvel that Steckler could bring in any kind of film on such budgets. The greatest marvel is that they are all entertaining, often bizarre movies, that seem to hold a funhouse mirror to genre filmmaking.

Steckler's preparation for the world of film was much like others of his generation. He started making 8mm films in his hometown of Reading, Pennsylvania, when he was 14 or 15 years old. He cast friends and family in them and generally had a good time learning the basics of filmmaking.

When he entered the army, he became a cameraman, learning the finer points of photography at Uncle Sam's expense. This experience would lead to his first work on a feature. After he had served his hitch, an army buddy asked him to be a camera operator on *Frenzy*, to be directed by Timothy Carey. The film would later be released as *The World's Greatest Sinner*.

His next assignment was a promotion, to director of photography on *Drivers in Hell*, an ultra-low-budget film that used his acting talents as well. Steckler's role required him to be in front of the camera for at least 50 percent of the film, in addition to handling camera and lighting setups.

Steckler's first big break was given to him by Arch Hall, who hired him to be his assistant on *Eegah!* a story about teenagers and a caveman, played by Richard Kiel (Jaws in the James Bond movies).

One day while shooting *Eegah!* on location in the desert, Steckler was performing the common chore of changing the film in a camera magazine. Hall had told him that they didn't have permission to use the land they were on. While Steckler stood off to the side carrying out his task, he saw a car approaching. An older man got out and walked over to him. It was the owner of the property.

Steckler tried to pass off what they were doing as "an educational film." Then the owner glimpsed Richard Kiel in his caveman outfit. It seemed that the jig was up.

The landowner proved to be very nice about it. "I used to make a few movies myself once in a while," he said. "I know what you guys are doing. But it's okay. Be my guest. Have fun, kid. Good luck in your career."

Steckler later found out, much to his amazement, that the landowner was Harpo Marx.

Hall decided to let Steckler direct his next picture, *Wild Guitar*. Again Steckler had to act in a film, as well as hold major duties behind the camera. The situation came about because Steckler had cast a black man in the role of the heavy. When time to shoot the picture drew near, Hall became worried that the film wouldn't be booked in the South if a black was in the cast. It was a sad time when Steckler had to tell his friend he wasn't in the picture. Then, having no one else on such short notice, Hall threw Steckler into the role.

It was the first time Steckler acted under the name Cash Flagg. The name was a kind of standing joke. Steckler was known for telling producers

Steckler worked as a theater usher while directing his first film *Wild Guitar*.

"pay me in cash, or don't pay me at all," having learned that the rubber check was a way of life in Hollywood.

Even with directing and acting, Steckler wasn't making much money in cash or in checks. He actually had to work as a theater usher while making *Wild Guitar*. Still, he gained experience as a director and was able to meet George T. Morgan. Morgan would become his producer for *The

What has to be the longest film title ever.

Incredibly Strange Creatures Who Stopped Living and Became Mixed Up Zombies. It was to become Steckler's best-known film.

Creatures is set in a world of carnival sideshows and seedy nightclubs. Whatever your suspicions are about such places, Steckler takes them a step further. Here we find that a fortune-teller is actually a murderous slave-master to a cage full of zombies.

The movie opens on a shot of a carnival. The camera makes its way to the tent of Madame Estrella, fortune-teller. Inside, Madame Estrella's

When a film had made the rounds, Steckler would rerelease it a year or two later under a new title. The best-known example is *The Incredibly Strange Creatures . . .*, rereleased as *Teenage Psycho Meets Bloody Mary*.

romantic advances on a half-drunk client are rudely rebuffed. Immediately, we get to find out just how she stocks her cage of zombies. Her henchman, Ortega, grabs the client, and they pour acid on his face.

Then, we cut to a small nightclub, where we see Carolyn Brandt, Steckler's wife in real life, doing a dance number on the small stage. Afterward, her character, Marge, retreats to her dressing room, where she begins to drink. We come to see her as a lost soul, with some terrible fate before her.

Fans will note on the dressing room wall a poster of Steckler's earlier film, *Wild Guitar*. The next part of the story to be introduced owes something to *Wild Guitar* and other youth films of the late 1950s and 1960s. In it, we are introduced to Jerry, a fellow who refuses to grow up and get a job. This is Steckler's role, which he played under his Cash Flagg pseudonym. We also meet his buddy, played by Atlas King. King was a likable actor, who had an unusual accent. Though he had trouble with English, the sincerity of his performance made up for any shortcomings he had.

Jerry and his buddy go to pick up Angela, Jerry's girl, for a night at the carnival. They go roaring over in an old beater of a station wagon. Angela's mother is not pleased to see Jerry pull up. In her eyes, Jerry will never amount to anything.

At the club, Marge has gone on stage drunk for her second show. She blows the dance number and gets a stern warning from her boss. It has a sobering effect on her. She consults her astrology guide and decides to get some professional help from Madame Estrella.

Madame Estrella deals the cards. The ace of spades, the death card, falls to the center of the spread. Superstitious, Marge is terribly frightened. She tries to run out of the tent, but loses her sense of direction, running into the zombie room instead. She manages to escape, but drops her purse. Madame Estrella finds it and knows that Marge has to be taken care of to keep her secrets safe.

Jerry and his friends see the girl run out. They decide they want to go in and get spooked, too. It is here that Madame Estrella spots Jerry. She will use him to take care of Marge.

After they leave the tent, Jerry becomes fascinated by the pitch for a girly show in the next tent. The spiel the barker delivers is great.

"Twenty beautiful girls, and only ten costumes! Like the Garden of Eden, but none of the trees have any leaves!"

Then, Jerry makes eye contact with Carmelita, one of the dancers on the platform. Jerry doesn't know that Carmelita is in league with Madame Estrella. He is completely captivated by her. He resolves to see the show, over Angela's protests. He winds up going in alone, his friend escorting Angela home.

The girlie show consists of several young ladies who seem to have just taken their first dancing lessons. While Jerry watches, Ortega brings a note to him from Carmelita, inviting him to come to her dressing room after the show.

Jerry goes behind the stage, looking for Carmelita. There, Madame Estrella has set a trap for him. When Jerry pulls the curtain aside, Madame Estrella is waiting on him with her amazing hypno-wheel. The hypno-wheel is only a disc with a spiral pattern painted on it, but it does the job on Jerry. He becomes a zombie, ready to do Madame Estrella's bidding.

She sends him to get rid of Marge. He does so, right on the stage of the nightclub, murdering her and her partner with a knife.

Jerry escapes and heads home. His sleep is filled with nightmares. (This sequence is one of the best Steckler has ever done.) When Jerry wakes from his tortured sleep, he remembers nothing of the murders.

He goes to Angela's house to try to make up. Angela is outside by the pool, a parasol in her hands. She is still angry, but willing to listen to him. But then as he talks, she starts to twirl the parasol. It triggers visions of the hypno-wheel, driving him insane. He starts to strangle her.

Angela's brother shoves him away. Jerry flees, wandering aimlessly through the city, trying to fathom what has come over him. He overhears a news broadcast about the murders. He decides to find Carmelita, to see if she can tell him what happened to him.

This is another bad move. Madame Estrella gets Jerry with the hypno-wheel again and sends him out to commit another murder. When he returns, she decides to add him to her cage of zombies. They splash acid on his face and start to shove him in.

But the zombies in the cage revolt. They come storming out, killing Madame Estrella and Ortega. They invade the girlie show and lay waste to the place, carrying off the women. The police arrive and start shooting the zombies.

Jerry comes out of his trance and makes a run for it. While all this is going on, his buddy has gone to Angela's to plead on his friend's behalf. Angela, her brother, and Atlas go out to search for Jerry, getting to the carnival as all hell breaks loose. They see Jerry run toward the ocean.

It is too late. Jerry motions for them to go back. He climbs a high cliff. As he reaches the top, a policeman shoots him. He falls to the bottom, dead.

Creatures boasts the talent of three of the best cinematographers in the business: Laslo Kovacs, Vilmos Zsigmond, and Joe Micelli. It should also be noted that the part of Madame Estrella is played by Bette O'Hara, who had worked for years as Susan Hayward's stand-in without getting a chance at a role. This was O'Hara's first picture. Steckler was able to manage all this on a budget of only $38,000, an amount that has proved to be his biggest budget to date.

Creatures got the "live monster" treatment at some theaters. "You will be surrounded by monsters," the posters warned. Ushers dressed like zombies would run into the audience at some point in the film and make menacing gestures toward the patrons. This was hazardous duty for the ushers because more than one got his lights punched out. Steckler himself was in several of these live monster shows, once getting shot with a pellet gun. It happened at a showing of another Steckler film that used the live monster gimmick, *The Maniacs Are Loose*, which is better known by its original title, *The Thrill Killers*.

The Thrill Killers may be Steckler's best film and certainly contains some of the best cinematography, thanks to Joe Micelli. Shot in black and white, the movie often has a film noir look. It stars Liz Renay, who had just been released from prison, having been put there for refusing to testify against her boyfriend. When Steckler heard she was getting out, he immediately found a place for her in his film, perhaps hoping for a publicity boost.

The Thrill Killers opens with a helicopter shot of Hollywood. It cuts to a street-level view, where we meet Joe Saxon. Joe, the narrator tells us, "is caught in the web of nonreality."

The opening narration alone makes *The Thrill Killers* worth the price of an overnight rental. The narrator goes on to explain the web Joe is caught in. Joe can't accept that he isn't a success as an actor. He's in debt up to his ears trying to live the Hollywood life-style. His wife, played by Liz Renay, was once an actress, but she has turned away form Hollywood and wishes her husband would.

Then the film cuts to Dennis Kestekian. The narrator informs us he is "caught in the web of reality." He has a modest home, with a yard full of kids, and a wife. As a new citizen of the United States, he is struggling to make a life for himself and his family.

Now, as any fan of Steckler's films can tell, the part of Dennis Kestekian is played by Atlas King, from *The Incredibly Strange Creatures Who Stopped Living and Became Mixed Up Zombies*. King's real name, as it turns out, is Dennis Kestekian. And the old beater of a station wagon he drives is the same one Steckler drove in *Creatures*. The wagon was Steckler's family vehicle. And the children in the scene belong to Steckler and other cast members.

The narrator has been building up sympathy for Dennis for a reason. While driving to work, Dennis spots a hitchhiker and pulls over to give him a lift. The hitchhiker is Mad Dog Click, played by Steckler. Click shoots Dennis without a care and steals his car, leaving him to die by the side of the road.

The staggering thing is that all this action happens before the titles come on. Talk about a fast-moving picture. And the entire film is like that.

Steckler's *The Thrill Killers* had some surprisingly intense moments.

It is crammed with action and lots of interesting people. After the titles, the film cuts to a Hollywood party, attended by Steckler's former boss Arch Hall, and his boss for that picture, George Morgan. They criticize Joe Saxon at his own party, while freely partaking of his booze.

This party is a little more than Joe's fed-up wife can take. She decides the next morning to slip away to her cousin's diner. It puts her right in the path of Click and his fellow escapees, who have just busted out of the hospital for the criminally insane.

Click has proved himself just as handy at killing with a pair of scissors as with a gun. He stabs a dance hall girl to death in her room, as the neon sign outside flashes off and on.

The rest of his gang prove handy with axes, guns, and whatever else they can get their hands on. They kill a young couple who stumble onto their hideout, splitting the man's head open with an axe and then going after the girl. As they kill the girl, the camera focuses on Herbie, one of the gang members, who pacifies himself by listening to nursery rhymes on the girl's transistor radio.

As in most such pictures from that era, the good guys win, and Mad Dog Click comes to a bad end. Steckler wanted to do a scene of his character being shot, then tumbling down a hillside into a pool of water. His character had tumbled down the cliff to the water in *Creatures*, and he would do the same in *The Thrill Killers*. The only trouble was that there was no water for him to fall into. That didn't stop Steckler. The crew dug a hole and filled it with buckets of water that they carried to the site. Click came to a bad end, and Steckler got his scene.

A film that may be the purest example of what Steckler is about as a filmmaker is *Rat Pfink a Boo Boo,* partly written by and starring his friend, Ron Haydock. Haydock's original script was entitled "The Depraved." It was the story of the kidnapping of a rock star's girlfriend.

Well into shooting the film, Steckler got a sudden brain wave. He decided to have Haydock and costar Titus Moede step into a closet and pop out as Batman and Robin—or at least his version of them. He got them some long underwear, stuck them on a motorcycle, and away the movie went. The script for the rest of the film was thrown to the winds as impulse and inspiration ruled.

Steckler didn't care what he put his actors through. He threw Haydock and Moede into a convertible and made them ride in a real parade, in their underwear costumes, so he could get footage for the start of his movie. He follows this scene with "rare documentary footage," as the narrator describes it, of Rat Pfink and Boo Boo meeting those they protect. What this is, is more home-movie footage of Steckler's and the cast's children, as in *The Thrill Killers*.

Then, the action switches to scenes they made for *The Depraved*—

chain-wielding psychos chasing a woman down a dark street. It is scary stuff.

We also find out about Lonnie Lord, the character Haydock plays. The narrator tells us he "sold ten million records last year." Not bad. "Everywhere he goes, he carries a guitar with him, because he never knows when he'll be called on to sing." If this isn't a song cue, I don't know what is. Sure enough, we find ourselves watching a proto-rock video of "Runnin' Wild." There are a lot of these scenes sprinkled through the film. In one, a girl in a bikini is wearing a zombie mask from *Creatures*.

Steckler didn't have to make obvious references to his other films. *Rat Pfink* is filled with artifacts from them. The old station wagon that popped up in *Creatures* and *The Thrill Killers* is in *Rat Pfink*, too, as is the truck the bad guys used in *The Thrill Killers*.

The bad guys start making crank calls to Lonnie's girlfriend Ceebee Beaumont, played by Carolyn Brandt. Finally, they kidnap her and demand $50,000 ransom.

In response, Lonnie sings, "I Stand Alone," while Titus tries to recover from the vicious attack made by the bad guys, one of whom busted his head with a claw hammer. But Titus is tough. He sits there with a bag of ice against his head. No hospital for him, even though the guy hit him hard enough to kill a mule.

It was at about this time that Steckler got his brain wave. So, into the closet Lonnie and Titus went. When they came out, they were crime-fighting superheroes. When they cranked their Ratcycle, it sounded like a toilet flushing. From here on, there would be no rules, no script, just some of the wackiest fun you'll ever see.

Steckler had wanted to call the film "Rat Pfink and Boo Boo," but the guy who did the title cards goofed. When Steckler found out how much it would cost to get the title fixed, he decided to let it go.

Impulse seems to be a big factor in Steckler's career. While lecturing at the University of Nevada at Las Vegas one day, he gave himself a challenge before the students. He would go out with his 16mm camera and shoot a scene in an alley using only two lights. He would take it back to class and let them figure out how he did it.

The resulting scene looked so good that Steckler decided to add more to it, eventually coming up with a feature. The only problem was that there was no dialogue in the entire film: He had shot a 72-minute silent movie. There being no market for such a film, he dubbed in a few lines of dialogue and added some narration. The result was *The Hollywood Strangler Meets the Skid Row Slasher*.

Steckler directed the film under the pseudonym Wolfgang Schmidt. He had decided to start using the name years before, when his career was at a low point. Steckler had become depressed. His films were poorly distributed, and nothing seemed to be going right. He told Ron Haydock that the name Ray Dennis Steckler had such a negative influence that he could leave prints of his films on the corner of Hollywood and Vine, and no one would bother to steal them. So they tried it: They left the films on the street corner, each clearly labeled with Steckler's name, and went away. An hour later they came back. The films had not been touched.

Steckler was convinced. He adopted the Wolfgang Schmidt moniker for at least three films: *Blood Shack, Revenge of the Ripper,* and *The Hollywood Strangler Meets the Skid Row Slasher.*

Ray Dennis Steckler is everyman with a dream. He has demonstrated his unique talent on pocket-change budgets because that's all he's ever had to work with. Yet no matter what limitations have been placed on him, he has always created entertaining films.

3

Humble Origins: Big-timers with Skeletons in Their Closets

Careers of the great and famous don't always have noble beginnings, particularly in motion pictures. Many an actor or director had their start in modest little films about bug-eyed aliens or some such thing. Steve McQueen in *The Blob* comes fondly to mind.

There's nothing wrong with getting your start in a movie that somebody made over a long weekend or, for that matter, making a career out of such movies. How would we know Tor Johnson without all those no-budget films they were grinding out in the late 1950s?

What's particularly juicy, though, are those films the big names would like to keep hidden. It's a kick to know that certain people with distinguished bodies of work did a sleaze film or something equally out of character. Just as interesting are stars who turned to exploitation films in attempts to revive their careers. Here is a mixture of both.

Francis Ford Coppola: Admirers of Coppola would have you believe that Coppola's first film was *Dementia 13*, that sometimes stylish, little black-and-white horror movie from the 1960s. But that isn't the kind of film that would qualify him for a chapter like this.

You have to go back to his true first feature. Hold on to your rompers, sleaze fans. Francis Ford Coppola, maker of the *Godfather* movies, started out with a nudie film!

The name of this priceless gem is *Tonight for Sure*. Coppola shot it in 1961, while going to film school at UCLA. This wasn't a student project. Coppola was out to try his hand in the newly born nudie genre and hoped to make some of the easy cash it was generating.

The picture was shot on a shoestring, like most nudies. Coppola took his camera to various striptease joints on the Sunset Strip. He patched together the feature, which was then scored by his father, Carmen Coppola.

One youthful indiscretion is pardonable, you may say. But what if I

This man, best known for directing *The Godfather*, started his career with a nudie, *Tonight for Sure*.

told you that Coppola made two of these things? He followed up *Tonight for Sure* with *Bellboy and the Playgirls*. The topper is that segments of the film are in 3-D.

The film was originally shot in West Germany in 1958. It was a showcase for famous British striptease queen June Wilkinson. The distributors wanted to take advantage of the flurry of interest in 3-D in the early 1960s. They hired Coppola to shoot some 3-D footage and then edited it into their film.

Sophia Loren: Has there ever been a woman as beautiful as the young Sophia Loren? Perhaps you remember when her movies first started to appear on American screens. There was one you didn't get to see for a while—until about nine years after it came out. It seems there was a bit of a censorship problem.

Two Nights with Cleopatra was the name of the film, and Sophia Loren had the title role. It was 1954. They had made a comedy in which nobody cared about the jokes.

Not that it wasn't funny. It was often delightful. The trouble was that the audience was in a state of nervous anticipation. You see, Cleopatra (that is, Sophia Loren) went skinny dipping in the film. Who cares about comedy when Sophia Loren is going to do a buff shot?

Naturally, the movie did big business in Europe. Nine years later, when the U.S. censorship codes had been knocked down by Bibo, Meyer, and the rest, *Two Nights with Cleopatra* would come to the United States. By then, Ms. Loren was a major star.

Some stir was created by the film's release here. Though the film is innocent by current standards, it was big news then.

Karen Black: Karen Black has stated that she's not embarrassed by anything she has done in a film. That she has continued to do nude scenes in movies would tend to back that up. But there was one film that embarassed her so much that she had her agent ask for part of the footage to be destroyed before it was released.

The movie is *The Prime Time*. It was Ms. Black's first appearance in a feature and H. G. Lewis's and David Friedman's first attempt at producing a film. (See Chapter 4 on H. G. Lewis.)

The movie was aimed at the young drive-in crowd. It was a typical 1960 movie about rebellious youths, delinquency, and a beatnik called "The Beard." It doesn't sound like anything to cause embarrassment. However, Lewis and Friedman, in an effort to draw crowds, went a step further. They pulled the old exploitation trick of throwing in a skinny-dipping scene. Though it was shot in such a way that the audience saw very little; nevertheless, Ms. Black could be glimpsed momentarily, according to reports.

In the days following, she began to have doubts about what she had done. So did her agent. Ms. Black was obviously talented. There was no reason to trip up a promising career right at the start.

The agent went to Lewis and Friedman and offered them a deal. In exchange for the footage of Ms. Black in the offending scene, he would pay for a full day's shooting with another actress. The two accepted the deal, being gentlemen—and smart businessmen. They didn't need a full day's shooting to replace the footage. The pair actually made money on the deal.

Jayne Mansfield: It seems that most big names become involved in exploitation at two points in their careers: very early or several years later, after thay have had a taste of fame and see it start to slide away. Jayne Mansfield belongs in the latter group.

Ms. Mansfield deserves special status in the hearts of exploitation fans. Whereas some are downright ashamed of their naughty little efforts, she never was. She worked to publicize those last exploitation films just as hard as she had any of the rest. She truly saw them as an opportunity and tried to do her best by them.

Yet when the name Jayne Mansfield is brought up, the general public never associates it with *Promises, Promises*. They call her "a second-rate Marilyn" or think of her tragic death in an automobile accident. It is all terribly unfair.

Unlike some others, Jayne Mansfield seemed proud of her exploitation efforts and worked hard to promote them.

At her best, as in *The Girl Can't Help It*, she was as good as any of them. The times then led people to compare her to Marilyn Monroe, but a far closer comparison could be made to Mae West. Mansfield didn't have the vulnerability of Monroe. She was sure of herself, had goals, and set out to accomplish them. She was considerably aided in her efforts by her I.Q., which was over 140.

Despite her early success, her career went into a gradual decline in the 1960s. Hollywood's taste was changing, and the "blonde bombshells" were on their way out. Jayne Mansfield could see this as well as anybody. Her response to it would be a bold one.

Nudity might not be acceptable at most theaters, but art houses and a few daring operators like Tom Dowd were showing skin flicks. Jayne decided these films were where the future was.

She accepted a role in the low-budget comedy *Promises, Promises.* Tommy Noonan would direct and star in the role of Jayne's husband. Mickey Hargitay, Jayne's real-life husband, would play the husband of Jayne's friend in the film. The film was set on a cruise ship, where the two couples would spend their vacation.

The film was no different from any of a number of similar films made in the 1950s, except for the two minutes or so of nudity featuring Ms. Mansfield. Otherwise, it was just a good-natured farce that was a little short on laughs.

Fans of trash documentaries have made a cult item of *The Wild, Wild World of Jayne Mansfield,* which was apparently assembled during a European vacation that Ms. Mansfield took. In the film, she visits the Isle of Levant nudist colony and other racy spots. They should have called it "Mondo Mansfield."

She didn't actually go nude for this film. Rather, they pulled some outtakes from *Promises, Promises* and showed the famous Mansfield issue of *Playboy.* However, what most people remember about the film is its ending. In amazingly bad taste, even for an exploitation film, the producers showed photos from the accident scene where Jayne died. They took a laughably bad documentary and turned it into something disturbing and sad.

Mamie Van Doren: Perhaps you think it a mistake to include Mamie Van Doren in this group. After all, her career was spent in exploitation films. But like the rest, a part of her career has been mostly ignored by those who have turned her into a major cult figure.

Her fans remember her for *High School Confidential,* in which she played Russ Tamblyn's oversexed aunt. Fanatics of bad movies love her in *The Navy vs. the Night Monsters.* But those of us who like to look under rocks and peek into closets have *Three Nuts in Search of a Bolt.*

This sex comedy can be blamed on Tommy Noonan, the same fellow who brought us *Promises, Promises.* It was the same sort of no-budget affair that relied on a similar gimmick: Viewers are treated to the sight of Mamie taking a champagne bubble bath.

Ms. Van Doren has proved to have a remarkably good attitude about her exploitation past, granting interviews and even appearing as the Queen of Teen in Rhino Video's Teenage Theater series.

4

H. G. Lewis: More Than Gore

Herschell Gordon Lewis is known as "the Wizard of Gore." He even made a movie with that title. His *Blood Feast*, shot in 1963, was the first of its genre. Yet for a man so identified with bloody excess, it's a surprise to find that more of his films either contained no gore or didn't use gore as their selling point than those that did.

Lewis's first film, *The Prime Time* (1960), was typical exploitation fare for those days. A young girl falls in with a fast crowd and is menaced by a deranged beatnik artist, known as "the Beard." Deranged beatniks seemed to turn up in a lot of films back then.

Acting only as a producer for this film, Lewis learned some hard lessons about the movie business. He hired the Fred Niles Studio to make it, rather than make it himself, even though he owned sufficient equipment. Why he didn't make it is hard to figure because he had a considerable background in industrial films and television.

There were many roadblocks to the production. The lines of job demarcation at Niles were so tightly drawn that a cable left unplugged could halt production until the proper person was found to plug it in. Gordon Weisenborn, a completely inexperienced director, and scriptwriter Robert Abel, who had no credits to his name, were hired because they were Niles's friends.

The only noteworthy points about the project were Karen Black's screen debut in a brief role and the fact that it was Lewis's first feature.

Lewis followed *The Prime Time* with *Living Venus*, a movie about a Hugh Hefner type who starts a magazine called *Pagan*. In this movie, Lewis applied some of the things he learned from the first film. He decided not only to produce the film, but to direct it as well. The film's plot had the obvious sex angle, but contained no nudity. This racy little black-and-white movie continued to get playdates ten years after it was released.

Living Venus starred the beautiful Danica D'Hondt as the title character. It was also the first appearance of William Kerwin in a Lewis film.

Kerwin is an icon of 1960s exploitation films. Known for his role as the police inspector in *Blood Feast* and as one of the two surviving tourists in *Two Thousand Maniacs,* he has appeared in more Lewis films than any other actor. He has acted under the name William Kerwin; Bill Kerwin; Thomas Wood; and, though it isn't widely known, Thomas Sweetwood. The Sweetwood name was used only in the nudies he did for Lewis.

Neither of Lewis's first two films was financially successful. This left Lewis and his main partner, Dave Friedman, casting about for a project. Any project would do, as long as it brought in some money.

Friedman met with Rose LaRose, the owner of a burlesque house in Toledo, Ohio. She routinely showed ten-minute segments of a movie between live acts, usually a feature that had a few glimpses of nudity somewhere in it. But what her audiences really liked were little self-contained short subjects, each having some pretty, naked girls. Could Friedman and Lewin concoct a few short films?

Friedman one upped her, promising a feature made of ten-minute segments, each self-contained. She was won over immediately.

Back in Chicago, Lewis and Friedman hired Billy Falbo and, Lewis says, "eight of the ugliest girls ever." It was a shoestring production all the way. Lewis would handle the camera, and Friedman the sound. They bought only 8,000 feet of film to shoot the entire project. At least it was color film, and 35mm.

This was how *Lucky Pierre* was born. Although there had been nudist camp films, and Russ Meyer had spawned the first nudie-cutie with *The Immoral Mr. Teas,* Lewis and Friedman were certainly helping to break new ground. Though the number of theaters that could play it was limited, it still made a handsome profit for them. It did so well for Rose LaRose that she gave up showing live acts and started showing movies full time.

Lewis had an advantage over other filmmakers in that he owned the means of production. While others had to rent cameras, lights, and all that went with them, Lewis owned everything he needed. It knocked his production costs way down.

The centerpiece of his outfit was a Mitchell NC camera, regarded as a workhorse in Hollywood through several decades. Though it had some miles on it, the camera was in top operating condition. This camera, when in its soundproof blimp, weighed so much that it cracked wooden tripod legs on more than one occasion. Lewis also owned a Cineflex and a Bell and Howell Eymo camera.

He acquired a second Mitchell without really trying. When a rental equipment company in Chicago wanted to go out of business, the owner called Lewis and asked if he wanted to bid on the company's Mitchell. Not needing the camera, Lewis made a bid so low that the owner laughed at it. A while later, the owner called back. Lewis's bid took the camera.

H. G. Lewis: Known for gore films, he pioneered several exploitation genres.

Between the nudies and Lewis's well-known gore films came a little picture called *Scum of the Earth*. This story, of a gang of pornographers and a young woman they deceive into posing for them, has recently popped up on video. It has been called a transitional film because it contains brief glimpses of nudity, along with a fair amount of violence.

Poster for one of the first roughies: *Scum of the Earth.*

Poster art for *Blood Feast*. Lewis made just as many films without gore as he did with it, but gore is what he is remembered for.

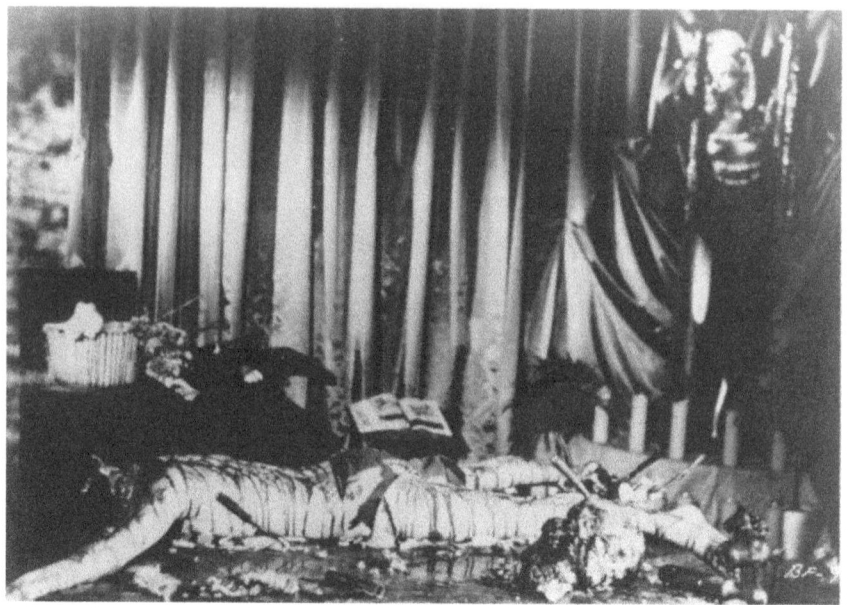

The lair of the deranged caterer Faud Ramses, and one of his victims, in *Blood Feast.*

The version that is out seems to be a general-release print. Some of Lewis's nudies came out in two versions, a general-release print to show at the drive-ins, which contained little or no nudity, and a specialty-house version, which was a true nudie film. *Scum of the Earth* may be a two-version film, but material about it is so scarce that it's hard to say. There are parts of the movie that appear to have been "plugged in," a giveaway that some kind of editorial high jinks have taken place.

Bill Kerwin plays a photographer for the porno ring, who turns out to be a good guy by the end of the film. He used the Thomas Sweetwood name for this movie, more circumstantial evidence that a nudie version may exist. Whether it does or not, the film is one of the earliest examples of the "roughies" genre that filmmakers like Russ Meyer cashed in on with *Lorna* and later movies.

In 1963, Lewis made *Blood Feast.* It had legendary drawing power, lining up drive-in audiences literally for miles. It played throughout the country, getting the widest distribution of any of his films. Each following installment of his gore trilogy, *Two Thousand Maniacs* and *Color Me Blood Red,* had a tougher time getting playdates. At the time *Blood Feast* came out, local censorship groups around the country were poised to jump on any film that contained sex or nudity. They weren't ready for the extreme violence Lewis dished out in *Blood Feast.* While it slipped by, anything

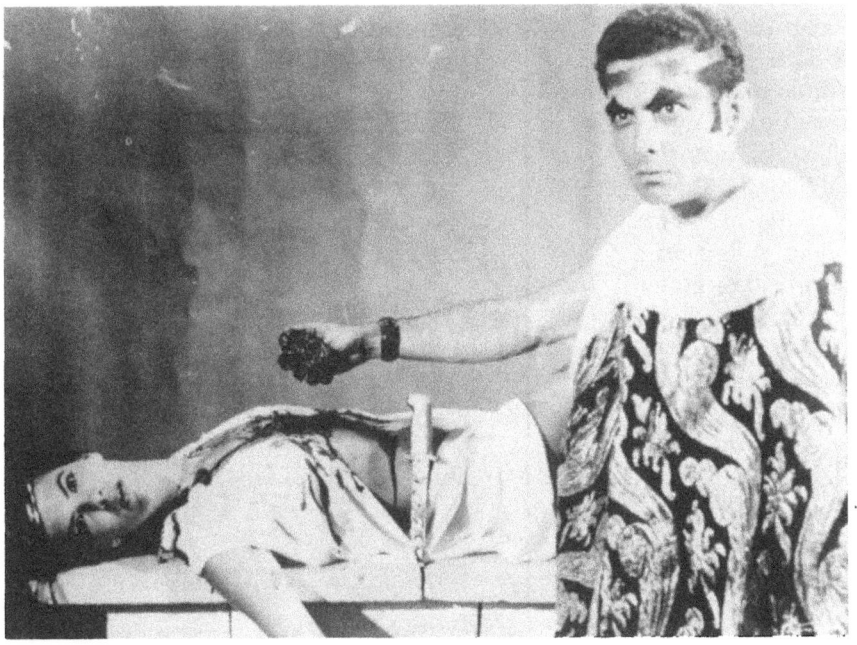

Jerry Eden had only a bit part in *Blood Feast*, but would star in several of Lewis's early nudies.

afterward was bound to get a going over. To get his films played, Lewis would have to try a different genre.

Taking into account the popularity of his films with Southern audiences, Lewis decided to tailor-make a movie for them. He came up with *Moonshine Mountain*, a story about a country western singer who goes home for a rest, only to become entangled in the activities surrounding the biggest illegal still in existence.

Chuck Scott played the singer and wrote the screenplay under the name Charles Glore. Adam Sorg, who was the insane artist in *Color Me Blood Red*, took the role of the sadistic sheriff in this film. Continuing to cast from his stock company, Lewis gave the part of the patriarch of the Carpenter family to Jeffrey Allen, who played the town mayor in *Two Thousand Maniacs*.

Lewis wasn't entirely willing to give up his macabre tricks in this film. There were some gore and violence, though not nearly as much as in the "gore trilogy," and gore wasn't used as a selling point for the movie.

Lewis attended a preview showing of the film at a Florida drive-in. As he watched the cars rolling in, he was disturbed to see so many young children in them. The film's ad campaign had been for a "good ol' boy" movie, saying little about the film's more violent aspects. Lewis quickly went to the projection room and edited out some of the most objectionable material, including a shot of a pair of boots being pulled off a corpse. The crowd watched and enjoyed, none the wiser of Lewis's act of conscience.

On the same double bill with *Moonshine Mountain* was a true cinema oddity, *Monster a Go-Go!* Bill Rebane, exploitation filmmaker, was at the start of his career when he tried to make the film he called *Terror at Halfday*. He ran out of money two-thirds of the way through the project. With no money and no answers, he shelved the film and tried to get on with his life. Then Lewis came along.

Lewis took

Monster a Go-Go! was the strangest film Lewis ever released. It came out on a double bill with *Moonshine Mountain*.

what Rebane had done, added a few transitions to move the story along, and gave it the most absurd narration possible. It wasn't much of a movie, but it served the purpose Lewis needed it for, just something to put on the road with *Moonshine Mountain*.

During the mid–1960s Lewis made a pair of ESP films. The first was *Something Weird*. James F. Hurley, an associate of psychic Peter Hurkos, came to Lewis with the script. It tells the story of a man who has been horribly scarred in an accident involving high voltage wires that took away his looks, but gave him ESP. A witch he meets gives him the chance to regain his appearance if he promises to love her.

Lewis did the best he could with the material. Hurley took the producer's credit on the film, but in reality, Lewis did the work. This project led to the second ESP film, over a year later, known as *The Psychic*. Hurley decided he would direct this one. *Something Weird* had not really said what he wanted to say about ESP. Lewis and his crew were hired for production duties.

The first-time director created a dull, unwatchable film that no distributor wanted. Hurley sought Lewis's help to save his film and his considerable investment.

Lewis told him that the cheapest solution would be to add some softcore scenes, so the film could play the grindhouse circuit. Hurley added one. Still, no one wanted *The Psychic*. More softcore scenes were added, and the film's name was changed to *Copenhagen's Psychic Loves*. It hit the road and played for years, making Hurley a modest profit.

Perhaps the most interesting thing about the movie is its schizophrenic trailer that displays the movie's two titles. The film itself is just as confused. It's a mess that Lewis doesn't deserve to be blamed for.

Suburban Roulette was the first of a group of films Lewis made that were considered risqué for their time, but aren't even as steamy as today's daytime soap operas. The film's subject, "wife swapping," was in the popular press at the time and gave it box office power. It's mostly remembered today as being one of the last two films Bill Kerwin made with Lewis. The other is *A Taste of Blood*, a vampire story shot the same year.

Suburban Roulette pointed the way for two other Lewis projects: *The Girl, the Body, and the Pill* (talk about high-concept titles) and *The Blast Off Girls*, a film about rock and roll groupies. These films mark the beginning of Ray Sager's stint with Lewis, for whom he worked as an actor and on the crew. Sager's career reached its peak when he played the title character in *The Wizard of Gore*.

Exploitation filmmakers around the country cashed in on the public's fascination with biker gangs in the late 1960s. Lewis only made one entry in this field, but it is a classic: *She Devils on Wheels*.

Allison Louise Downe, who contributed to many of Lewis's productions over the years, got real women bikers as actresses. These women were members of the Female Cut-Throats Division of the Iron Cross motorcycle gang. Downe used connections she had developed as a probation officer to acquire their services.

The film had all the conventional biker movie scenes, but with women riding the big bikes, beating people up, and generally raising hell. Overall, it is one of Lewis's best pictures and is second only to *Blood Feast* at the box office. It played in some areas on a double bill with the first Billy Jack film, *Born Losers*. It should be noted that Lewis's film got the percentage of box office receipts, while *Born Losers* was booked at a flat fee.

She Devils on Wheels starts with a good girl, Karen, leaving home in her car. But she's not in a car for long. She parks it in a garage and comes roaring out on her motorcycle.

Every weekend the Man-Eaters have a race at an abandoned airstrip that they have claimed as their territory. The race isn't to see who has the fastest bike. It's to get first pick from the stud line, a group of men who come to their parties for the orgies afterward.

By this point in the film it's plain to see that Lewis has taken the macho biker fantasy and turned it inside out. In this film, the women were the sexual aggressors, and the men had become the "mamas" to be tossed aside after sex.

But Karen, who wins the race, doesn't quite conform to the Man-Eaters code. Every week she picks the same man, a fellow named Bill. When she does so again, it draws the rest of the gang's attention.

The gang's leader, Queen, calls the gang together. They don't like what they've seen of Karen. She will have to be put to the test.

The next night, a strange sight awaits Karen. Bill is tied behind her motorcycle. For her to stay in the Man-Eaters, she is forced to drag him behind her bike, around and around the airstrip. He is skinned alive by the pavement.

Next follows a staple of the biker movie, an initiation scene. Honey-Pot is a teenage girl who hangs out with the gang. She's not as tough as the rest, so they take her in as a kind of little sister. The ceremony devolves into a drunken rampage through town.

The next Saturday, a gang of male hot rodders has taken over the airstrip. The Man-Eaters won't put up with it. They take hold of the men and start beating them up. This isn't one of those scenes in cheap exploitation films like *Superchick*, in which it's obvious that the women couldn't possibly be whipping the men; in *She Devils on Wheels* the women look and fight like they could kick the crap out of anybody. And they do. The hot rodders leave, defeated.

But the men won't let things lie. They decide to take their revenge by kidnapping Honey-Pot. The scene in which they plot it out has the strangest feel of reality to it. Were the male actors letting their feelings of embarrassment, at having to play roles that had them bested by women, seep through?

They brutally beat Honey-Pot and stick a ring through her nose. They leave her near the Man-Eaters clubhouse with a note, telling who was responsible, dangling from the ring.

Whitey, the biggest of the Man-Eaters, and another member of the gang go to vandalize the car of the hot rodder's leader. He sees them at it, which was just what they wanted. Whitey jumps on her bike and cranks up, ready to escape. Her gang mate can't get her bike to crank, so she jumps on with Whitey, and away they go.

The hot rodder manages to crank the bike they left behind and takes off after them. But it was all part of the Man-Eaters' plan. They've stretched piano wire across the road, right at neck level. He rides into it and is decapitated, his head flying through the air.

Queen loses her belt at the scene of the wreck. It seems that the police will have them. But by some unexplained means, they beat the rap and go free. Lewis had thumbed his nose at convention through the entire film, so why change at the end?

Just for the Hell of It was made by Lewis on the same trip to Florida when he made *She Devils on Wheels* and shares some cast members. This seldom-seen picture about a gang of teenage vandals was way before its time. It would have fit punk mentality perfectly.

During the late 1960s, the adult film market shifted from nudies to softcore. Lewis made several of these films, none of them particularly noteworthy. All of them were done on the cheap, often for Tom Dowd, owner of the Capri Theater in Chicago.

Lewis did at least two of these films in southern California, which led to a bizarre coincidence. One of the films was a western, called *Linda and Abilene*. Needing a location, Lewis's project coordinator booked the Spahn Movie Ranch, not long before the Tate-LaBianca murders.

Safely back in Chicago months later, when full details of the Manson gang's activities became known, Lewis would reflect on the strange people who seemed to hang about the fringes of the set. No one had known who they were or had any hint of what would happen.

In the late 1960s and early 1970s, Lewis acquired the services of some well-known show business personalities. He used Henny Youngman in *The Gore Gore Girls* and Tim Holt in *This Stuff'll Kill Ya.*

This Stuff'll Kill Ya was to be Holt's last picture; he died shortly after the film was completed. In it, Holt played Federal Agent Clark, assigned to investigate a moonshine ring. Lewis brought back one of his stock company favorites, Jeffrey Allen, to play Preacher Roscoe Boone. Boone's Holy Roller church was a cover for the moonshine ring.

Lewis decided to shoot the film on location in Oklahoma City and Chakota, Oklahoma. He used an abandoned UHF TV station for some interiors and for the set of Roscoe Boone's church. Lacking a proper projection room to view the rushes, Lewis and his cast would head down the road each night to the Highway 69 Drive-In and watch them after the movie was over.

The script called for car chase scenes. Lewis arranged to shoot them on a gravel road that couldn't be blocked off at both ends, so the crew was never really sure if a car was coming from the other direction. When the brakes froze on one car, Lewis told them to cut the brake lines. He then climbed in with the camera, and they took off. Lewis got the shots he wanted.

Year of the Yahoo starred Claude King, the country singer who had a pair of hit songs, "Wolverton Mountain" and "Tiger Woman." King played a singer who falls into the hands of political media flacks, who want the honest and folksy King to run for office and see him as ideal material for their exploitation.

This was perhaps Lewis's only attempt at a serious, mainstream type of movie. It boasted a three-week shooting schedule, the longest of any of his films. He was rewarded with a finished product that looks as good as most studio films, at a fraction of the budget.

A series of financial reverses in the early 1970s, not connected with his films, put Lewis out of movie production. His last film, *The Gore Gore Girls* was completed in 1972.

There have been persistent rumors that Lewis could resume filmmaking. One deal to make *Blood Feast 2* fell apart at the last minute. For those of us who enjoyed his films, I can only say I hope Lewis will again take up his cameras, whether for film or video, and give us at least one more.

5

Russ Meyer: T and A and $

"Is she woman . . . or animal?"
"So much for any woman . . . too much for most men!"
"Get a good grip on your popcorn!"

I think the last line is good advice for anyone who goes to see a Russ Meyer movie. These quotes from his ads tell no lies. Meyer delivers what he promises, to the delight of his fans and the mortification of bluenoses everywhere. Meyer's work is obsessed with the female bosom. And not just any common specimen of this part of anatomy. He has sought out superwomen, like Tura Satana, a former stripper, to make into his stars. He created the "nudie-cutie" genre when he made *The Immoral Mr. Teas.*

Yet, this same man keeps surprisingly sentimental mementoes from his early life and military days. He has devoted small "shrines" in his home to dead comrades from these times. He organizes reunions of his old buddies from World War II, acting as a sort of unofficial leader and memory keeper for the gang.

How did this obviously complex man get started in filmmaking and come to pick the subject matter that he has? (Which, by the way, goes far beyond the nudie material it seems to some.)

Meyer was born on March 21, 1922, in San Leandro, California. His father was a policeman, and his mother worked as a nurse. Somehow, she was able to set aside enough money from her salary to buy young Russ a movie camera when he was 14. It was a Univex Single 8 that retailed for $9.95. That may seem humorously cheap when compared to the price of the camcorders desired by today's teenagers, but in the Great Depression it was money hard come by. The projector sold with it cost $14.95, and a roll of black-and-white film went for 60 cents.

Meyer's life revolved around that camera and learning the craft of cinematography. Before long, he would win a prize in a national contest for amateur filmmakers. The prize, and all the work he was doing, would lead to the first major chapter in his career: his days in the army.

Rather than handing him a rifle and telling him which way to shoot, the army had a different kind of shooting in mind for him once it learned of his talents. He was assigned to the 166th Signal Photographic Corps and was sent to Europe as a cameraman.

Here the Meyer mythos begins to form. In an interview on "Entertainment Tonight," he claimed that his first trip to a French brothel was financed by Ernest Hemingway. More important than his sexual high jinks was the work he was doing. Meyer filmed Patton's advance into Germany, some of it on color film. Color was rare for documentary work then, particularly in films done by the military. The footage was so good that some of it was used in the movie *Patton*.

Meyer truly loved life in the army and the thrill of documentary work under the toughest conditions. He was making friends, like Dan Ornitz and Bill Teas, who would stay friends for life. But all through this time, he was plagued by one particular worry. He wasn't afraid of being shot or captured by the enemy; he was dreading the end of the war! The thought of the kind of job he might have to return to, when compared to this, the kind of life he wanted to lead, was a miserable one for Meyer.

He was ready to go to Japan if the chance offered itself and cover the invasion that everyone in 1945 believed was coming. Then, the bomb was dropped, and Meyer's career as a combat photographer was over.

What Meyer feared would happen at the war's end did. He had to go back to a job he didn't like—one that was utterly unsuited for a man of his temperament. The workaday world just wasn't for a man who saw life the way he did. He craved excitement, but not just for its own sake. It was creatively interpreting events, while somehow keeping himself alive in the middle of the biggest war the world has ever known, that was the magnitude of challenge he sought.

Above all, cinematography was still his love. He decided to try for a job in Hollywood, but found almost every door closed to him. The jobs in Hollywood were strictly union, and Meyer wasn't a member. Men who had held cards in the union before the war were returning home and would have first crack at any work that was available. Meyer was only 19 when the war broke out, far too young for a fellow with no connections to have gotten into one of Hollywood's most exclusive unions.

But a fellow who lives on challenges the way he did couldn't be kept out entirely. Meyer found work as a still photographer at the big studios. For this, he didn't need to be a union member, and his background was sufficiently impressive to win assignments. He did stills on some of the most famous movies of the day, including *Guys and Dolls* and the classic, *Giant*, starring James Dean.

He was around films and in Hollywood, but it still wasn't what he wanted. Filmmaking was the only thing that would satisfy him.

He moved to San Francisco and started making industrial films. Companies like Standard Oil and Southern Pacific were glad to hire so talented a man. The films were used to train employees and, in some cases, as public relations tools. They followed the framework of the documentary, the medium Meyer loved. His work was at the highest level of professionalism and helped bring him more assignments.

It was at about this time that Dan Ornitz, his old army buddy, suggested that he try shooting nudes for the calendar and girlie magazine market. At the time, the field was wide open. Models were hard to come by, the morality of the 1950s being what it was. Many of the photographers were hacks, unable to bring anything to the work beyond technical skills.

Meyer gave it a try. Soon, he was one of the biggest names in the field. The pinups he did for calendars were some of the most popular in the country, and the rather modest girlie magazines of the day sought his work. Hugh Hefner got some of Meyer's best work for the first issues of *Playboy*. This material is now traded as if it were gold.

Meyer made industrial films and shot pinups for about four years. He enjoyed what he was doing, but wasn't completely satisfied. Still, he might have continued with it, were it not for the urgings of a friend, Pete De Cenzie.

De Cenzie owned a burlesque theater. At that time, the burlesque houses kept their doors open from the beginning of the first show to the end of the last. A fellow could walk up at any time, pay his admission, and go in. Some sort of entertainment was always being presented. Keeping a show on for 12 to 14 hours was difficult, and keeping live entertainment on stage that long was just about impossible. More than anything else, it was the cost of so many acts that drove theater owners to seek other solutions.

One solution they had used for years was the burlesque film. Often it was just a filmed version of striptease acts, but a few of the films had a thread of plot woven in. The trouble with burlesque films was that the supply was so limited.

De Cenzie encouraged Meyer to make a burlesque film that he could show in his theater. De Cenzie also provided a contact with one of the top names in burlesque, Tempest Storm. Meyer went ahead and shot the film that De Cenzie wanted, using Ms. Storm as his star.

Meyer had made a fine film, but one that was behind the times. Burlesque films were being pushed aside in the marketplace in favor of the nudist film. De Cenzie tried to get Meyer to follow up his initial effort with a nudist film, by Meyer was uninterested.

To Meyer, the genre was simply too dull. The films were rather sexless creations, aside from the nudity itself. Almost all of them had a large part of their action set in a nudist camp, where endless scenes of people enjoying the healthy life-style the films promoted were shot. There were scenes of people playing in the pool, the traditional volleyball games, and a lot of people carrying guitars. If one is to judge by the number of people in these films with guitars, then nudists must be the most musical people on Earth.

The plot for most of these movies was almost always the same. A person, either skeptical or against nudism, is exposed to the life-style and is won over by the end of the film.

There was nothing there for Meyer. For him, the ideal film would have his type of woman, the large-bosomed Valkyrie, involved in a truly erotic story. Making such a film would just be asking for trouble. While the nudist and burlesque films contained nudity and Hollywood products contained a certain amount of eroticism, neither contained both. A film with any dramatic impact, containing nudity, would call too much attention to itself.

Getting attention, even in the burlesque theaters and specialty houses that showed nudity, meant trouble. For these theaters the ideal film was one that kept their regular customers pleased, without bringing them into the glare of public scrutiny, where some bluenose could use the opportunity to close them down.

But Meyer sought to make just such a troublesome film. Perhaps he wanted to dull the edge of any critic's argument about his film's daring content by making it a comedy. It is also known that he was an admirer of the French film *Mr. Hulot's Holiday*. Probably more than anything, Meyer's rather sardonic sense of humor led him in this direction.

Whatever the reason, he'd have to pick a project that he could shoot cheap. He wrote a script about a fellow who goes to the dentist and has a fairly unusual reaction to the anesthetic: It enables him to see through women's clothes! The movie would be narrated with bawdy, often hilarious remarks.

Meyer told some of his old army buddies about the project; they pitched in a good part of the tiny $24,000 budget. He even cast his old army pal Bill Teas in the lead, lending his name to the title: *The Immoral Mr. Teas*.

The film they shot, in only four days, had a totally professional technical approach. Meyer's perfectionism, which had served him well in the past, would allow nothing less. More important, he had translated his funny story to the screen successfully. He was again proving himself to be more than a good technician. He was a truly creative filmmaker.

The Immoral Mr. Teas was head, shoulders, and other body parts ahead of the nudist films. It drew crowds, big crowds, wherever it was shown. It also drew the attention of censors, bluenoses, and the law.

The movie was dragged into courtrooms across the country. Newspapers made much of the fight, helping to swell the box office take. Meyer was doing so well, it didn't matter if the courts hassled him. The money was rolling in.

Of course, when exploitation filmmakers see one fellow have a success, dozens rush to imitate it. Without intending to, Meyer had created a new genre: the "nudie-cutie."

Meyer followed his success with several more humorous, naughty little films over the next five years. One, *Eve and the Handyman*, starred his wife, Eve, who eventually gave up acting to become her husband's associate producer. Other films during this period included *The Immoral West, Erotica, Europe in the Raw*, and *Heavenly Bodies*.

All genres — horror films, westerns, skin flicks — go in cycles. The length of a cycle is usually determined by one factor: the box office. Meyer could see the revenues from his films steadily tailing off because of many factors.

One factor was that there were simply so many nudie-cuties out there that the public's taste was sated. More competition meant that fewer booking dates were available. Many of these films were awful "bandwagon" movies that drove away all but the hardiest skin flick fans.

Tough competition was beginning to come from Hollywood. While they were not brave enough to show nudity yet, movies like *Tom Jones* served up erotic story lines; humor; lots of cleavage; and, hardest of all to beat, big-studio production values. The innocent little nudie-cutie, with its four- or five-person cast, shot at somebody's vacation cabin, was doomed.

Here, an intriguing turn in Meyer's career would occur. Though most credit Meyer with having a kind of inspiration to add violence to his films, cold calculation may be closer to the truth. A look at certain other exploitation filmmakers shows why.

Years earlier, when Meyer had hit big with *The Immoral Mr. Teas*, H. G. Lewis and Dave Friedman jumped in with *Lucky Pierre* and followed it with an assortment of nudist camp pictures and nudie-cuties, like *BOIN-N-G!* They, sooner than Meyer, saw the declining box office trend begin to develop.

Faced with facts, Lewis and Friedman made a transitional film called *Scum of the Earth*, which had all the elements of the next wave of exploitation: beautiful girls, some the victims of graphic violence, and the sleaziest male characters imaginable. Rather than follow up on this film's modest success, they took the angle of violence, strongly graphic violence, for their next film — the ground-breaking *Blood Feast*.

Did Meyer note the high box office receipts of *Blood Feast*, as Lewis and Friedman had his *The Immoral Mr. Teas,* and decide that the violent approach was for him? Of course, this is all speculation. In truth, most entertainment was becoming more violent, but not so straightforward as Meyer would be. This was his real inspiration. Meyer's next cycle of films would deal with sexual frustration, lust, and sadism. It would start with the film *Lorna*.

Continuing his habit of using the star's name in the title, *Lorna* starred perhaps the most beautiful of all the women Meyer has used in his films, Lorna Maitland. Ms. Maitland would also do *Mudhoney* for him the following year.

In *Lorna,* she plays a young woman whose sexual desires are unfulfilled by her husband. She loves him and he loves her, but his needs are filled by their once-a-month trysts. She needs more, but is too repressed to tell him.

Then one day while walking in the woods, she comes across an escaped convict. In one of the most objectionable sequences in a Meyer film, the convict rapes her, and she finds sexual gratification in the experience. She takes him home with her for more lovemaking. When her husband returns, there is a tremendous fight, and Lorna is accidentally killed.

The whole film seems to come off saying that since Lorna had sexual desires, she had to be punished. That none of this is to be taken seriously, Meyer telegraphs to the audience, particularly through the character of the Preacher. The Preacher shows up at various points in the film, warning of the doom they all face because of their actions. The guy is a loony.

Though *Lorna* wasn't the first of the "roughies" genre, it was the most successful of the early ones, and, as with most Meyer films, it drew a raft of imitators. Filmmakers might be able to copy his nudie-cuties and do a fair job, but no one was able to make a roughie with the same verve that Meyer could.

Many critics think the best film from this period in Meyer's career was *Faster, Pussycat! Kill! Kill!* It starred Tura Satana, a tall, beautiful brunette, who was big enough and tough enough in this film to be intimidating. She plays Varla, leader of a group of three women who like to spend their spare time driving fast cars flat out across the desert highways.

In a fight after a race with a man, Varla uses karate to break his back. The scene is convincing because Satana was a karate expert in real life. The gang leaves the man to die, deciding to kidnap his girlfriend.

They stop at a gas station and hear about an old man and his sons who live on a ranch not far away. Supposedly, the old man is keeping a large sum of money that he won in an insurance settlement hidden on the property.

Varla decides she has to have the money. They go to the ranch, ready to use whatever means necessary to get it. But the old man turns out to be just as evil as Varla. The lecherous old man, played by Stuart Lancaster, tells his hulking son Vegetable that they can bury the girls in the desert after they've had some fun with them.

The action is as wild as anything seen in a Meyer film. One unusual point is that there is no nudity in the movie. All attention is directed toward the story and performances, which are exceptional.

The movie did well at the box office when it was first released, like most Meyer films, but after a while it was forgotten. For years it would be overshadowed by other Meyer films in the minds of his fans. But one fan wouldn't let it lie in obscurity.

John Waters, himself an exploitation legend, loved *Faster, Pussycat! Kill! Kill!* He collared all who would listen to him and told them about the film. Finally, in his book *Shock Value*, he had the chance to turn a wide audience on to the movie. He said it was the best movie ever made and that Meyer was the Eisenstein of sex films. Waters's book started such a large cult following that the movie is probably Meyer's most popular film.

The movie that led to the biggest change in Meyer's career was *Vixen* (1968). Meyer used a backwoods setting and kept the cast fairly small. It meant he could also stay with his typically low budget, only $76,000.

The movie did something no one could have predicted, not even Meyer. It went through the roof at the box office, bringing in $7.5 million in its initial release. *Vixen* started getting playdates not only in drive-ins and art houses, but in first-run theaters as well. Suddenly, Meyer was competing with the major studios, and beating them. *Vixen* became one of the most talked-about films of the year, and Meyer himself was getting serious attention from the critics. In the title role of the film was Erica Gavin. The plot tried to deal with her character's political awakening, but the movie was really about sex. Meyer eased off on the violence, creating a movie less objectionable to women and thus possibly increasing the number of couples who came to see the film.

As *Vixen* drew people into theaters, the major studios began to send out feelers to Meyer. They were hungry for hits, seeing their established directors serve up one dud after another. Most of all, they wanted the youth market, which seemed to have deserted them in favor of freewheeling, often experimental, independent films. Among Meyer's fans were the college-age crowd, drawn to Meyer by his outrageous stories and humor.

Though the heads of the big studios might not understand what an independent like Andy Warhol was up to when he pointed a camera at a building for eight hours, Meyer's films they could see into. Since his films were about sex, they should give him a really big sex picture to direct. Then they'd get the youth market and make a bundle of money.

That was just what 20th Century–Fox had in mind. And it had the sequel rights to a really big sex picture, *The Valley of the Dolls*. The studio signed Meyer to direct the sequel for release in 1970. Roger Ebert, now one of America's most famous film critics, but then just starting to make a name for himself, was hired to write the script.

Ebert liked both Meyer and his movies. The two of them decided that *Beyond the Valley of the Dolls* would be the ultimate Meyer film. The movie would be a carefully crafted outrage.

The idea immediately ticked off Jacqueline Susann. She threatened to file a lawsuit if her characters or storyline were used in the film. Twentieth Century–Fox gave in, leaving Meyer with only a title to exploit.

This, of course, didn't faze him or Ebert for a second. They wrote a script about three young women who have a band called the Carrie Nations. The film follows their struggles in the music business and the bedrooms of Hollywood.

This film defies easy description. It seems to have every quality of every Meyer film up to that time, each cranked up to the maximum. There's humor, sex, violence, and wild plotting; in short, Meyer had succeeded in doing exactly what he set out to do.

So had 20th Century–Fox. The film raked in big profits for the studio and brought in the college-age crowds. The studio heads were ready to offer Meyer another film.

Yet, somewhere along the line the rot set in—not with Meyer or his fans, but with the critics. It seems that it was okay to like Meyer as long as he was perceived as an independent with a certain flair. He was a filmmaker those "in the know" could point to, recognizing his talent. It's always fun to be in the know. It gives the person a feeling of superiority.

But once Meyer was making studio pictures, the critics seemed to sour on him. You can't be in the know if it's something everybody knows about. Others were disappointed in the film itself. They'd hoped Meyer would use the chance to make an "important" picture. It seemed that getting the all-time, knockdown, drag-out, Russ Meyer movie wasn't what they were after.

Perhaps they were hoping for art. All Meyer had aimed to do was please, giving them everything he'd learned in years of filmmaking.

Then came *The Seven Minutes*. You can figure the studio logic here. "Meyer made a pile of money for us with one sex novel, so we'll give him another. Sure, he didn't use *Valley of the Dolls*, but think what he'll do when we give him a book he can use." He made a dud. No doubt there are filmmakers who could make a good movie from the Irving Wallace novel, with its courtroom scenes, its search for the true author of a pornographic novel, and its statement about censorship. Actually, Meyer probably could have, if given free reign. Such was not the case. So, Meyer decided to go his own way and became an independent again.

Blacksnake was his first try in this period. It was a blend of sex, sadism, and blaxploitation, set on a Caribbean island in the 1800s. A woman plantation owner, given to beating her slaves and having adventures in the bedroom, is killed by the end of the picture, her plantation burned when the slaves revolt.

Opposite: **Promotional art for *Faster, Pussycat! Kill! Kill!* featuring the cult star Tura Satana.**

It was a well-made film that somehow didn't connect with the right audience. Meyer now had two box office failures in a row.

An independent cannot last long if he loses money. To solve his problems, Meyer looked back to the time before *Beyond the Valley of the Dolls*. He wanted to make a surefire crowd pleaser. His answer was *Supervixens*, a movie featuring one big-breasted woman after another and lots of violence. It hit big at the box office. In coming years, he would make *Up!* and *Beneath the Valley of the Ultravixens*. These three films should be thought of as a group, just as the early nudie-cuties make up one stage; the roughies, the next; and the studio movies, another. While the earlier films were breaking ground to make a dollar, the movies from the 1970s seemed to be made in reaction to what was happening in the marketplace.

Not only did Meyer have the problem of back-to-back failures to overcome, he also had a new form of competition to go against. Hardcore porno was taking over in many of the grindhouses and "art" theaters. Although Meyer had legions of fans who had no interest in hardcore, the audiences did overlap. Worse, the wide-open days of the late 1960s and early 1970s, when any theater might book a Meyer film, were over. Meyer was stigmatized as a sex-filmmaker. Theaters that might have booked his pictures in the past closed their doors to him now.

Drive-ins, one of the most dependable markets for Meyer, were falling to the greed of real estate developers. Newspapers in some areas refused to carry ads for X-rated movies. It made no difference that Meyer's films weren't hardcore, they still refused the ad space.

Meyer was in a corner. Fewer theaters were around that would play his films, it was tougher to get the word out about them, and hardcore films showed more. He did have an ace in the hole. His name and reputation guaranteed to theater owners a certain number of ticket sales. If he delivered the goods with each picture, meaning a film with all the elements his fans expected, there was a good chance of financial success.

What he couldn't do was take a risk on another film like *Blacksnake*. Real experimentation was too great a risk. He could take the standard elements of his films and heighten each to a cartoonish level of intensity. But change the elements, the type of story he told, as he had when he turned from the nudie-cuties to the roughies, no.

Meyer seemed to sit out the 1980s, but this was a false perception. He was using the decade to produce a mammoth, multicassette video that will be released under the title *The Breast of Russ Meyer*. It will contain highlights from all his films, plus be a kind of video autobiography. The amount of new footage shot will outweigh the highlight portions, which means that the whole project will be of staggering length, considering some reports that Meyer is planning to use upward of 15 minutes from each of his more than 20 features.

6

Kroger Babb: Who Was America's Foremost Hygiene Commentator

What kind of a fellow names himself for a grocery store chain, makes the ultimate "birth of a baby" movie *and* a film of the Passion Play? Why, "America's most fearless showman," the notorious Kroger Babb.

Through the 1910s and 1920s Babb was a young man struggling to get by. As a boy in Wilmington, Ohio, he worked in a Kroger store. The other kids started calling him Kroger. Babb liked the sound of it so well that he dropped his first name, Howard, and was known as Kroger the rest of his life.

Kroger had a number of jobs early on, often as a carnival barker or some other sort of huckster. It quickly became apparent that he had the gift. Selling and promoting, with a fine line of talk, a smile, and a pat on the back, that was Kroger's life.

He wasn't going to stay a carnival barker for long. He soon became the manager of the Checkers chain of theaters in Ohio. While on the road one day, he took in a show at a competitor's theater, where there was a line around the block waiting to get in. Anybody who did this kind of business he had to find out about.

The movie was *Dust to Dust*. It was being promoted on a town-to-town basis by the two legendary roadshow agents, Cox and Underwood. The two got a print of the Bryan Foy picture *High School Girl* and added "birth of a baby" and VD reels. Where the cops were lenient, these reels would be shown as part of the film. Elsewhere, they would simply be left out.

Cox and Underwood were doing well with *Dust to Dust*, but Kroger thought they could do better. They didn't stand a chance when Kroger started his pitch to them. He was determined to get into the roadshow business. This kind of film was a chance to put everything he knew about promotion, which was considerable, to work. Kroger was the kind of man it was impossible to say no to. By the day's end, he was partners with Cox and Underwood.

It was a fateful move for Kroger. As they moved the film through the Midwest, drawing crowds and taking their money, they eventually came to Indianapolis. Here, Kroger would form another partnership.

One day, while Kroger was away from the theater, a woman named Marilyn Horn came to see the show. It was bad news for the theater manager. Miss Horn hated the show, thinking it immoral and filthy. She promised to close it down.

Her promise had weight to it. Her father and brother were policemen, and her uncle was a well-known preacher. All her family held positions of respect in the community. To add to all that, Miss Horn was the top movie reviewer of the city's newspaper.

When Kroger heard about what had happened, he resolved to see Miss Horn. Whatever he said to her, it must have been good. Miss Horn ran off with Kroger and spent over 30 years with him.

With her background, you'd think she would be the last person to do such a thing. Maybe you're thinking she spent all that time trying to reform him. Hardly. She wrote the script for the most notorious of all the "birth of a baby" films, *Mom and Dad*.

She and Kroger formed Hygienic Productions to make the film. As producer, Kroger hired William "One Shot" Beaudine to direct. Beaudine was an interesting fellow, known for cranking out B westerns literally by the hundreds. Beaudine was fast and efficient, seldom doing a second take, thus his nickname "One Shot."

Mom and Dad was shown to segregated audiences. There would be one show for the women and another show for the men. Though the ads might not say it directly, it was insinuated that this sort of material was too hot to be shown to a mixed audience.

The movie opened with a sing-along of "The Star Spangled Banner." Perhaps Kroger thought there was less chance of getting thrown in jail for a movie that started off with the national anthem. Or maybe he just wanted to throw in a little patriotism at a time when it went over well.

Once the story got started, it was pretty much the same as all the other "birth" movies. A young girl, through ignorance and parental neglect, gets pregnant. But Kroger had an additional gimmick.

Halfway through the film, an intermission was called. Then, Eliot Forbes, "America's foremost hygiene commentator," would step out on stage to lecture. The lecture was a sales pitch for a one-dollar pamphlet about human reproduction. These pamphlets sold like hotcakes. Of course, Eliot Forbes was a pseudonym. Actually, there were as many Eliot Forbeses as Kroger had prints in circulation. One of the best of the Forbeses was Scott Hall, a former carnival barker.

Then the lights would go back down, and the rest of the movie would be seen, including the "birth of a baby" scene that gave the subgenre its

A magazine ad for Hallmark Productions, Babb's company. It's goose that laid the golden egg was *Mom and Dad*.

name. This was color medical footage Kroger had bought from someone and spliced into the film. It did sort of clash, since the rest of the movie was black and white, but no matter. It played theaters for the next twenty years.

It's hard these days to understand the kind of turmoil this film caused. Of course, a lot of it was Kroger's own doing. A favorite gimmick of his was to hire vagrants to act like sidewalk preachers, denouncing the evil movie

Babb knew more about how to exploit films than anyone else in the roadshow game.

and urging people to stay away. To make sure that people stayed away, the preachers passed out handbills showing the exact locations of the theaters to stay away form and the show times. Some of the guys must have been real stemwinders. This little trick caused riots in Phoenix, New Orleans, and Hamilton, Ohio. The box office swelled.

Naturally, the Catholic church's Legion of Decency put the film on its condemned list. Kroger promptly announced that his next film would be *Father Bingo*, "a movie that would rip the lid off gambling in the parishes." *Father Bingo* was never made.

If you want to see what all the fuss was about, *Mom and Dad* is available on tape from Video Dimensions.

Kroger, a student of human nature, knew that although sex would bring people into the theaters, other things would do so just as well. He decided to turn from things of a carnal nature to those of a spiritual one. His next movie would be *The Prince of Peace*.

The Prince of Peace was a filmed version of the yearly Passion Play performed in Lawton, Oklahoma. It would be high-class stuff. There'd be no problems from the law or religious groups with this film. He could play the deep South, where religious feeling ran high, and the money would come rolling in. Besides, an Oklahoma oil company was offering $10,000 to film the Passion Play and distribute it. This was a tailor-made opportunity.

Yet when everything seems so good, there's always a catch. People came to see *The Prince of Peace*, but walked out halfway through. This had never happened to Kroger before. He got Dave Friedman, who was often a partner of his, to take a look at the film and try to figure out what was wrong.

When the first actor opened his mouth, it all became very clear to Friedman. The twangy Oklahoma accents were killing the picture. Not even Southerners wanted to hear the Gospels interpreted with a heavy dose of "y'alls" and "a-gonnas."

Kroger hired radio actors in Atlanta to dub a new voice track for his film. It helped considerably, but there were a few little details that nothing could be done about. For example, on the way to Calvary, power lines can be seen in the background. A few anachronisms wouldn't stop Kroger, however. He prepared a new ad campaign and sold lithos of Christ and miniature Bibles at the screenings, and soon the money did roll in.

It didn't always work that way. Two of his films flopped at the box office. *One Too Many*, a story about alcoholism and drunk driving, didn't make it. The exploitation angle here was that it was about women alcoholics, a subject previously not given much screen time. Unfortunately for Kroger, this reasonably well-made film just wasn't sensational enough to draw an audience.

The Secrets of Beauty failed not in its concept, but in its choice of product. Kroger made a film designed to be a kind of feature-length commercial for a ten-dollar beauty kit he sold at the theaters. The trouble was that few women could afford to pay ten dollars for makeup in those times. It was an interesting experiment that years later would come to dominate certain kinds of television, particularly children's programming.

Kroger's next big winner was *She Shoulda Said No*, an entry in the "good girl goes bad after one puff of marijuana" genre. It starred Lila Leeds.

Lila Leeds was notorious for her part in the Robert Mitchum drug bust of the late 1940s. It was Leeds's apartment that Mitchum had gone to that night. Out of nowhere, police burst in and found a small amount of marijuana. It had the look of frame-up from the beginning.

Frame-up or not, Mitchum did six months at the work camp. Leeds also did some time in prison. After she got out, Kroger grabbed her for this film. He even had her doing anti-marijuana lectures in the theaters. You can get *She Shoulda Said No* from Sinister Cinema. It also stars Lyle Talbot and Jack Elam, at the start of his long career.

Kroger decided to go the documentary route in the 1950s. He bought African footage from a Los Angeles dentist named Truetle and entitled it *Karimoja*. Notorious for its blood-drinking sequence that had viewers sick to their stomachs, *Karimoja* stayed on the road longer than any other of Kroger's films, except *Mom and Dad*. Paired with it was the short subject *Halfway to Hell*, a collection of Holocaust footage, narrated by Quentin Reynolds.

Perhaps the most unlikely pairing of names is that of Kroger Babb and Ingmar Bergman. Yet Babb did get the rights to a Bergman film. Babb had no high-minded motives of bringing art to the drive-ins. The film had a glimpse or two of nudity in it. He cut out the slow parts and retitled it *Monica: The Story of a Bad Girl*.

7

John Waters: They Used to Call Him "The Prince of Puke"

Picture a youngster putting on puppet shows at birthday parties. See the early innocent yearnings for show business success. He distributed flyers to drum up bookings for his show.

A little later, you can see him dance on the television program "The Buddy Deane Show." The show was a kind of teenage dance and music program, similar to "American Bandstand." He was a face in the crowd, one of the guest teenagers who helped fill up the floor, not one of the important regulars. He danced with one of the Deane show regulars at a country club dance contest, and they won. He proved himself to be as good a dancer as anybody on the show.

This fellow sounds like an all-American youth. So how did he wind up making movies about people who eat dog poop?

He was lucky. Most other fellows with this kind of background, coming out of the 1950s and early 1960s, would have wound up toting a rifle in Vietnam. Or maybe going to college and hoping for a high draft lottery number when he got out. When all was said and done, a promising career as an accountant or a Ford salesman would be their lot in life.

But not John Waters. Here, some serious warping of the mind was going on. It was happening at the local theater.

This was the golden age of exploitation, and Waters was determined not to miss a title. His heroes were men like William Castle, who pulled in the crowd with gimmicks like "Percepto," which was used to promote *The Tingler*. Percepto sent a faint electrical shock to the posteriors of people sitting in specially wired theater seats. Waters went to see the film, figuring on getting zapped. The catch was that only a few seats would be wired in any given theater. Not wanting to miss out, he spent the first part of the film hunting about the theater for a wired seat.

There were others. Russ Meyer was a special case. Although Waters hadn't been a fan of Meyer, *Faster, Pussycat! Kill! Kill!* really did the trick. He was lured to a nearby drive-in by the film's radio ad. It promised to "leave a taste of evil in your mouth." That sounded okay to him.

Waters was hooked by the film. He went back the next night, and the next, and the next. So what if he was sitting in a car by himself in a drive-in. He was a young filmmaker, and he was being influenced.

That the film wasn't getting the attention it ought to bothered Waters. He went out of his way to get his friends to see it. Later, when he became famous, he would write a book called *Shock Value* and spend a good part of it promoting the movie. He called Meyer "the Eisenstein of sex films" and patterned characters in his own films after those in *Faster, Pussycat! Kill! Kill!* (with female impersonator Divine in the Tura Satana roles!).

No budding young sleazemonger of that time could ignore H. G. Lewis. Lewis taught an important fact to anybody who cared to notice: You don't have to make a polished film to draw people into the theaters. If you are outlandish enough, if you are daring enough, you can have a hit film. Waters noticed, and then some.

To be any sort of filmmaker requires knowledge of the craft. Waters was lucky in that he was growing up at a time when film schools were starting really to teach filmmaking, with an eye toward placing people in the business. He selected NYU and seemed to be well on his way.

His career at NYU lasted a remarkably short time. Depending on who you ask, he either dropped out (NYU's version) or he got thrown out (Waters's rather frank admission).

So where was the luck? Waters was never meant to be an NYU kind of filmmaker. Can you see him applying for governmental grants to do a film about some serious subject? This is a fellow who idolized William Castle. This is a fellow who was born for exploitation.

Since his attempt at film school was a failure, he had to teach himself how to make movies. In the 1960s that meant a Bolex camera and gathering up all your friends to use as actors. He shot short films with titles like *Hag in a Black Leather Jacket* and *Eat Your Makeup*.

Though these early attempts show the influence of his exploitation idols, they more closely resemble avant garde films of the day. Waters has long preached the gospel of sleaze, but he has spent a fair share of his life in art theaters.

He admits that as a teenager he would play hooky to see Ingmar Bergman films. For many of his fans, this might be as jarring as finding out that Mother Teresa was a closet Charles Bronson fan.

Some of his other idols from the art film world, they can understand. Pier Paolo Pasolini, certainly. Any filmmaker who used so much depravity in his works seems sure to be a favorite of Waters. Later, he would admire the brief but highly productive career of Rainer Werner Fassbinder.

While Waters was making his little 16mm movies, a new genre of filmmaking was getting under way. *Mondo Cane*, a documentary that promised to "take you beyond the pale," was doing great business. It spawned a wagon load of imitators, all graphic and nasty.

By 1969, Waters decided to make his own "mondo" movie. It would be feature length, a first for him. That fact alone meant he would have to raise some cash. A short film could be made for whatever he had in his pocket at the time shooting began, but a feature meant buying at least a case of film stock.

He was able to scratch up about $2,000, which would buy a lot of black-and-white stock back in the 1960s. Rather than film tribal rites in darkest Africa, he would pick a far more dangerous place: Baltimore, his hometown.

Mondo Trasho begins with a real shot of chickens getting their heads chopped off. This repellent scene is enough to turn many people off to Waters immediately. Yet this is the only truly "mondo" element in the film. The rest of the movie is a bizarre comedy about what happens after Divine accidentally runs over a young woman. Waters didn't even shoot the chicken scene. It was existing footage that Waters found out about and bought.

A $2,000 budget doesn't allow for many extravagances. Things like a sound track, for instance. Dialogue was out of the question because sync sound equipment just wasn't available. He would have to make do with music. Fortunately, he possessed an extensive record collection that he was able to use in dubbing. If it was legal to do so or not, who knows? The stuff he used may have been in the public domain. At any rate, he got it for the right price: free.

Publicity, of the free sort, would help get the film booked. The script called for Divine to be eyeballing a nude hitchhiker when she runs over the girl. To get the shot required having some guy stand naked by the side of the road. This bit of monkey business had neighbors calling the cops. Waters and his crew were busted.

The idea of a movie with a nude hitchhiker was surefire newspaper material. The mostly conservative press was certain the country was going to hell in a handcart, and this was just another sign of it.

This might have been enough to make a success of the film, but the movie was just too crudely made to get booked outside of a few art theaters. Waters's breakthrough film was still a ways off.

Multiple Maniacs wasn't a breakthrough, but it was a step up technically, though just barely. Waters managed to shoot this one with sync sound. He was finally able to arm his characters with the wild, often funny dialogue that future films would take better advantage of.

The title of *Multiple Maniacs* is a homage to H. G. Lewis and his film

2000 Maniacs. The plot, however, is entirely Waters's, with his fascination for front-page crime stories; it was based loosely on the Sharon Tate murders. In the film, Divine owns the Cavalcade of Perversion and Traveling Freak Show, which contains such sideshow acts as a puke eater and two homosexuals. These exotic sights lure in middle-class types, who Divine robs and murders.

Waters's lack of funds really shows in the first sequence, where we see the freak show. It is made up entirely of tents of the sort you might take camping with you. Curiously, this actually adds to the film. Fans of backyard cinema get to see a genuine example here.

Divine's character becomes increasingly insane. She commits mass murder in a living room, providing the tenuous link to the Tate murders. By now, she is totally gone. She hallucinates being raped by a giant lobster.

Multiple Maniacs did get more bookings than *Mondo Trasho*, but really couldn't be looked at as a success. Waters's films seemed limited to viewings in a few art houses that appealed to an anarchistic crowd. It would take desperate action to get his career going.

He went to Divine and said something along the lines of, "Look, you want to be famous, and so do I. It's time to stop fooling around."

Waters began to outline the most extreme, disgusting things he could think of—things that had never been put on the screen before. He was well schooled in the art of exploitation and knew what others had tried. He also knew that the first film of a type could break the box office, the way *Blood Feast* or *The Immoral Mr. Teas* had.

His genre would be bad taste, and his taboo would be almost unspeakable: an authentic scene of someone eating dog excrement. Divine would get to do the honors.

They certainly had stopped fooling around. Anyone who was willing to eat dog poop to become a success probably needed something other than success. He needed a doctor. But considering the gang that Waters made films with, many of them with drug habits and even worse problems, eating dog poop probably was a small offense.

If you've got someone who is willing to eat dog poop, you don't want to waste it with cheezy 16mm black-and-white cinematography. Waters figured this was time to go all out, and color film was the answer. Shooting color meant getting a lot of cash together—about $12,000. Where he got it, nobody knows, but he did manage to come up with it.

For a title, Waters selected a symbol of bad taste, *Pink Flamingoes*. The lawn ornaments would be stationed prominently outside the trailer where Divine and her family in the movie live.

In the movie, Divine claims the title of the world's filthiest person. The Marbles, played by David Lochary and Mink Stole, covet the title. They

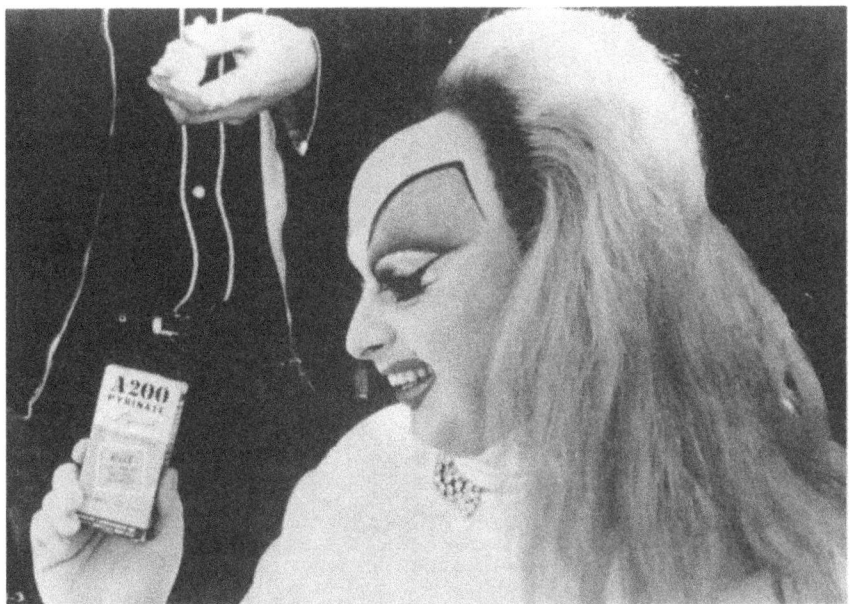

Pink Flamingoes established Waters and Divine (pictured) in the world of exploitation films.

have a substantial claim in that they kidnap women, have their butler impregnate them, and then sell the babies. They also sell drugs to schoolchildren and put money into porno scams. Certainly not the sort of folks you want next door.

Divine's qualifications include prostitution, murder, and having the craziest family imaginable. Mama Edie sits in a playpen all day, fixated on eggs. Her son, Crackers, has one of the more peculiar fetishes ever committed to celluloid (except maybe in a south-of-the border porno loop): He has a thing for chickens. Cotton, played by Mary Vivian Pearce, is the only person in the family who comes close to being normal.

Waters showed all the production values his tiny budget would allow. He even burned down Divine's trailer. Admittedly, the thing was a trap, and probably was cheaper to burn down than to have towed away, but Waters was putting a lot on the screen with this scene. Hollywood filmmakers couldn't pay for firemen for a scene like this if they used his entire budget.

In the movie, Divine swears vengence on the Marbles, who burned her trailer. Earlier, they had angered her by sending her a turd in the mail. First a turd, then her trailer goes up in flames. Serious measures were called for.

Divine murders the Marbles before an audience of tabloid reporters.

Divine in *Female Trouble*.

That problem out of the way, the only one left is to clinch her claim to the title of the world's filthiest person. She does it with the scene that packed the theaters: She eats dog poop.

A lot has been said and written about this scene. Ignoring the usual outcries against public decency, the rest just wonder how they did it. Was it real?

Waters said they went following the little dog around all day, waiting for it to take a dump. When it finally gave in to the demands of art, cinema, and nature, Divine was ready. Supposedly, she just scooped it up and popped it in her mouth.

Years after the film was made, someone tried to claim that what Divine ate was actually a lump of peanut butter.

Say it ain't so.

Whether or not it was so, news of the scene spread fast. The film was ideal for the midnight movie circuit. Once booked into a theater, it often played there for years. People went back to see it dozens of times. Waters finally had his breakthrough hit.

Waters built on his success with his next film *Female Trouble*. He brought back most of his troop of actors for the film, including Divine. While *Pink Flamingoes* put Divine on the map as a personality, *Female Trouble* gave her the chance to establish herself as a real comedy actor/actress.

Divine plays the role of Dawn Davenport, who has a troubled time as a teenager. She gets into trouble in school for eating a meatball sandwich in class. Her dream is to own a pair of cha-cha shoes. When they don't materialize under the Christmas tree, Dawn decides to strike out on her own.

Now her troubles are really starting. She is raped by a horrible drunken man. Waters had a stroke of genius, giving Divine the rapist role to play as well. Only Waters would give someone such a double role, and only Divine could play it.

As a result of the rape, Dawn gives birth to a girl. Unable to support her child by normal means, she is forced into a life of crime and prostitution.

The owners of the beauty parlor she goes to have an unusual philosophy: They think "crime is beauty." According to them, Dawn can become the personification of this philosophy. They hire her to commit crimes while they take pictures.

She rises to the absolute zenith of beauty, in their eyes, when she gets the death penalty for all her misdeeds. By this time she has kidnapped, murdered, and somehow had the audience laughing through much of it.

This "crime is beauty" theme is a particular interest of Waters. His statement, "People always look better under arrest" was made in reference to his longtime interest in crime and court cases. For several years he has maintained a correspondence with a member of the Manson family. He thought about proposing marriage to one of them — not actually marrying her, just proposing. When a friend learned of his interest in the John Wayne Gacy case, he commissioned Gacy to do a painting for Waters. It was of the Wicked Witch, from *The Wizard of Oz*, one of Waters's favorite screen characters. Another fellow sent him a bottle of soil taken from Gacy's front yard.

Waters served up another dose of crime and misbehavior in *Desperate Living*. This film features one of the more bizarre murders Waters has ever had in a film, which is saying a lot. An immensely fat woman sits on a man's face and smothers him to death. The tone is set for the rest of the film.

There's a cop with a panty fetish, a nudist garbage man, and a lesbian who has a sex change and then decides to undo the operation with a knife; in short, whatever way you're twisted, there's something for you in this film. It has even got Edith Massey (Mama Edie from *Pink Flamingoes*) as the dictator of a town filled with criminals. For many, this film is the best of Waters's "bad taste" movies.

His career was now at a crossroads, much as it had been at the time just before *Pink Flamingoes*. Waters thought he had said all that he wanted to in this direction. Not that he was giving up on bad taste; it's just that he wanted to spread it to a wider audience than he had in the past.

Waters's movies had accomplished everything he had intended for them to do. They had rubbed people's noses in the most outrageous behavior and made them laugh at it, though it was a nervous laughter for most. People asked themselves, "Do I really think this is funny?" when confronted with one of Waters's often repulsive scenes. The majority said, "Yes" even if they did leave the theater shaking their heads at what they had seen.

They had also made Waters famous. He was sought after for interviews for magazines and newspapers. Talk shows of a certain stripe wanted him as a guest. Though he was not fabulously wealthy, he wasn't poor either and didn't have to struggle.

A legion of fans had been attracted by his films. Mostly they were young, fans of cinema who enjoyed the midnight showings the movies were often booked for. They reveled in Divine's antics, anxiously awaiting the next shock. They wanted more, crazier, wilder. They wanted every movie to top the one before it.

Waters was a cult director. The most famous one in the United States, but still a cult director. Every film he made was devoured by his fans, but you wouldn't send your Aunt Sally to see one of them.

His shock tactics had won him many fans, but prevented him from gaining mainstream acceptance. Although he may not have thought of this, or even cared if he had, it was the case by the late 1970s. And if he wanted to make better, more ambitious films, he would have to have this kind of acceptance.

Waters's films still had the rough edges brought about by low-budget production methods. No matter how much skill he gained, those edges would still be there until he got more money.

Some people may think this sounds like a sellout. Actually it was far from it. He was in danger of being trapped into making the same kind of movie for the rest of his career. Nobody wants to wind up at 70 years old making movies about people eating dog poop. He wanted to do something different, to move on.

His transitional film would be *Polyester*, the story of Francine Fishpaw, a woman trapped in an awful marriage, caring for an equally awful family. Waters's description of the film as *Father Knows Best* gone haywire is an apt one. Francine is, of course, played by Divine. Her husband runs a porno theater, her daughter is a sleaze, and her son is the weirdest sort of criminal—he goes around stomping people's feet. (Curiously, there is a documented case of a person with just this strange sadistic urge. Waters must have known about it.)

To escape this mixed-up life, Francine has an affair with Tod Tomorow, played by none other than Tab Hunter! Their kissing scene had to have rocked a lot of Tab's old fans who came to the theater just to see what he was up to after all these years. In the film, Tod is the antithesis of Francine's husband. Though he owns a drive-in, he plays only art films. One night there's a Marguerite Duras triple feature. (Duras is a favorite of John Waters.)

The bigger budget Waters had for *Polyester* shows. There are none of the rough edges that audiences saw in his earlier films. There aren't any little moments of mystery in the sound track when you can't exactly tell what a person says. And the bigger budget gave Waters a chance to salute one of his early heroes, William Castle.

Waters would have his own Castle-like gimmick for the film, Odorama. Patrons received a scratch-and-sniff card as they entered the theater. When a number flashed on the screen, they would scratch off the appropriate spot on the card. They would be able to smell exactly what Francine smelled. Naturally, Waters's devilish sense of humor had them smelling some pretty awful things. Today, a complete, unscratched Odorama card is a hot item among memorabilia collectors.

The coming of the VCR would give Waters's fans a chance to own their favorite titles and to see early ones that perhaps they had missed. Films like *Mondo Trasho* and *Multiple Maniacs* were difficult to see in theaters, unless you were able to catch a retrospective at an art house. Getting a distributor for such titles would not be without glitches, however.

Media Home Entertainment was set to release four of Waters's movies, when its midwestern sales force balked; to them, Waters's films were just too offensive to market. Considering some of the things Media sold, this view is kind of hard to figure. But they made their stand, and Media backed out on the deal.

Waters jumped on the opportunity for publicity. Soon, Continental Video came forward with a far bigger offer for these suddenly hot titles. Waters had won the exploitation game again.

With his transitional film *Polyester* and videos of his older movies coming out, Waters was in a position to break ground in a land he had never seen before, PG country. He might not be aiming for mid–America, but his dog poop days were behind him.

His search for a subject led him back to his own youth, dancing on "The Buddy Deane Show," and how the show captured a generation of Baltimore youths. *Hairspray* would be his first crossover hit, lifting him from the ranks of cult directors to someone Hollywood had to pay attention to.

In the film, Rikki Lake plays a teenager who rushes home every afternoon to see "The Corny Collins Show"—a dance program patterned after "The Buddy Deane Show." Though overweight, she dances energetically. Her friend says she ought to be one of the regulars on the show. They make plans to go to a Corny Collins sock hop.

At the hop, she is discovered and asked to appear on the show. She can Madison and do the Mashed Potatoes with the best of them. Her rise to teenage stardom begins.

Divine plays her mother. A favorite scene comes near the beginning of the film, when Divine accuses her daughter of being a "hairhopper." Who but Waters would remember this authentic bit of early 1960s slang?

Hairspray was a hit, not in midnight shows, but in suburban theaters and shopping mall multiplexes. Waters was now bankable, according to the Hollywood establishment. Financing was available for just about any project he wanted to try.

Waters would reach farther back into his youth, to the mid–1950s, for his next film. *Cry-Baby* is a musical, what star Johnny Depp called "*Grease* on acid"—a fair description. Depp plays the title character, a "drape," the prototype juvenile delinquent, with his hair greased back and a black leather jacket. Rikki Lake plays a pregnant teenager, and Traci Lords and Patricia Hearst play mother and daughter, in what has to be Waters's most controversial casting ever. With an $8 million budget, he could do these things.

And for old-time Waters fans, there was Mink Stole. She played a chain smoker. In an iron lung.

8

Trailers: Coming to This Theater

"Are you ready to see . . . life in the raw?" the screen asks.

Boy, am I! Bring it on.

"Are you prepared for your children to . . . attend unchaperoned parties?"

Heaven forbid!

"Then see *Marihuana: Weed with Roots in Hell*," or *Pin Down Girls*, or *Dance Hall Racket*, or . . .

Just how many films like these promised us "life in the raw" or something similar? Probably a hundred. How many of them came through? How many of them were ever as good as the trailer, that little preview clip every theater and drive-in ran with each show?

I'm just old enough to remember seeing trailers for wretchedly old films like the ones above at nearby drive-ins. They made my young child's heart yearn to see such rubbish, but I was almost never allowed to. It wasn't until I was grown that I got to see them. After I saw them, I realized what I really loved was the trailer, that little hyped-up, two-minute tantalizer, that was often way better made than the movie itself.

Lucky for me, there are a lot of trailer fans out there. Video companies have rushed in with dozens of collections to meet the demand. Rhino's *Sleazemania* tapes have set the standard, but other companies have caught up quickly. Video Dimensions offered *Drive-in Sleaze 1934–70,* a 55-minute tape. Recently, they've pumped it up to 100 minutes, adding loads of additional trailers, and retitled it *The World of Sleaze*. Sinister Cinema has at least three volumes of its *Exploitation Trailers,* in addition to collections of trailers of every type of movie. If you want to see them, they're out there.

Of course, every collection has its high points, those trailers that far outshine the rest. The following are descriptions of special "coming attractions," each of which is a delightful gem. Pay no attention to the order in which they're listed. Each is equally good in its own way.

The Smut Peddler: "You want to know how scummy people move around?" the old pervert asks. What I want to know is, who made this trailer? There is no more wonderful a piece of slime on celluloid than this little clip.

It starts out with the audience looking through a keyhole. We see a fat man sitting at a table. He is playing with dolls, talking to them. Then he spies us.

He yells out roughly, with an accent that is flavored with German by way of Brooklyn. At first it seems that he is trying to run us off.

"Everybody comes crawling on his hands and knees to try to get a glimpse inside my room," he says.

He must figure we are his kindred spirits (and if we weren't, we wouldn't be watching this thing in the first place) because after a moment, he welcomes us to watch.

"I have an open keyhole policy," he states.

"I was just about to put some sinful pictures in my family album," he says, by way of showing us some scenes from the movie. And with every scene he makes a comment.

You can imagine the scenes just by hearing his lines.

"Get a good shake for your money."

"...a man with a taste for the lowlife."

"...a girl with lots of spit, and no polish."

While the girls in this mid–1960s black-and-white softcore are pretty, I can't imagine anything in the film being as good as this trailer.

At the end, the pervert admonishes us: "Get your evil eye out of my keyhole. One eye is for amateurs. You're no amateur. See *The Smut Peddler* up close. Look like a man!"

See this trailer!

Often paired with the trailer for *The Smut Peddler* in these collections is one for *Strange Rampage*. This one features "Miss Ann Howe, and her 48s."

On hearing that line the first time, I almost fell out of my chair laughing. I do admit to glancing at Miss Howe, just to see if there was any truth in advertising. There might be—just might. The camera pauses to leer for a moment, then gallops off to other sights, such as Bunny Ware, Ann Howe's costar.

More important is the nighttime drive the camera takes through Miami. Here, for all you gorehounds, is a glimpse of Mecca. Yes, plainly visible, on the right-hand side of the screen, you can see the Suez Motel.

So what, you say? Maybe if it was the Bates Motel, now that you could get excited about. But the Suez Motel? What was that?

That, friends, was the Miami headquarters for Herschell Gordon Lewis and Dave Friedman. When they came south to make *Blood Feast*, that is where they stayed. That is where they filmed the scene in which Astrid Olsen gets her tongue ripped out. This place ought to be set aside as a national landmark.

In the film clip, you can even see the Sphinx and the Great Pyramid in front of the Suez that Lewis and Friedman used for the opening titles of the film. For the gorehound, those two seconds or so make the trailer required viewing.

Since *Strange Rampage* shares some of the same cast members as *The Smut Peddler*, I have to wonder if they were made by the same people. The ties don't end there. An old clipping of an ad I saw shows them playing a double bill. They were both shot in black and white. And, of course, they're both preserved together in the trailer collections.

For these softcore films, "skin flicks," to burst on the scene in the 1960s, a group of movies had to pave the way. They also had to win some important court cases. Everyone remembers Russ Meyer's *The Immoral Mr. Teas* and the court battles it had to fight. But one film before it plowed just as tough a row, Walter Bibo's *Garden of Eden*.

Bibo's film was a nudist camp movie. It wasn't the first. By the late 1950s, several of them were floating around, usually playing burlesque houses if they played anywhere. Bibo didn't want to play his film in the strip joints; he wanted to put it in legitimate theaters. Burlesque houses booked films at a flat rate, usually $200 a week or less, whereas theaters paid a percentage, so theaters were where the money was.

Besides, Bibo was something of a crusader. He truly believed he had the right to show his film wherever there was an audience willing to pay for it. He went to New York with a team of lawyers and a pocketful of cash, ready to battle the censor boards.

When the case came to trial, Bibo's argument was simple: Nudism was an activity practiced by thousands of people. It was not lewd or lascivious, but a healthy life-style. As such, he had the right to document it on film and show the film to the public. After a drawn-out fight, Bibo won. He could show *Garden of Eden* in New York.

What he perhaps hadn't foreseen was that every distributor that owned a nudist camp film was primed and ready to jump into New York if he won. No sooner did *Garden of Eden* open than it had competition. Much of it was lousy. Every old scratched-up black-and-white pensioner that could run through a projector was trotted out. Even 1933's *Elysia*, by Bryan Foy, was booked.

Garden of Eden had them beat on several counts. The women were good looking, and everyone was really naked. This wasn't one of those deals where the cast was always standing behind bushes or a fence. You could actually see them. A beachball might be strategically placed; otherwise, there was skin.

Was it great drama? Of course not. Again, for modern audiences the trailer is what you want to go for. Actually, the trailer is a kind of condensed version of the movie, one of the best types of trailers.

It starts with one of the funniest moments in the film, when the film's lead actor sputters into the telephone, "I'm surrounded by naked people."

Just by watching the trailer, we can see that the rather staid gentleman learns to loosen up and by the end of the film will be won over to nudism. This would be the simple plot that every movie producer would copy for the dozens of such films that would come out in the next few years.

Making these little films is an art form, and there are companies that specialize in cutting trailers. Producers send them workprint, and they do the rest. Most exploitation filmmakers either couldn't afford such services or wouldn't trust something so important to somebody else.

If a producer wanted to cut his lab costs to the bone, he could use his outtakes to assemble a trailer. This way he wouldn't have to pay the lab to duplicate footage used in the film itself. After all, if you have two equally good shots of something exciting, why not get some use out of both of them?

Trying to cut corners does have hazards. A clear example is the trailer for *The Psychic*. The movie was released under two titles, the one just mentioned and *Copenhagen's Psychic Loves*. Somehow, they both got left in the same trailer. A full explanation of this blooper appears in Chapter 4.

In the collections of trailers that are available, men like Lewis are well represented. Among other favorites is Phil Tucker, director of that classic 3-D bomb, *Robot Monster*. His *After Midnight* series surfaces in the *Sleazemania* tapes. *Bagdad After Midnight*, in which "a bevy of temple virgins dance to the Sultan's command," comes across as an ordinary strip film. But the *Tijuana After Midnight* trailer is funny, thanks to the addition of a couple of baggy-pants comics.

One of the strippers wants to be wooed by one of the comics. When she asks him, "But do you have ze guitar?" well, you'll just have to see it.

Other "don't miss" trailers include the one for Tucker's *Dance Hall Racket*, with Lenny Bruce and Ed Wood star Timothy Farrell. You've heard about *The Man from U.N.C.L.E.*? How about *The Girl from S.I.N.*? There's Dwain Esper's *Maniac* and both versions of *Marihuana: Weed with Roots in Hell.*

I Married a Savage has "the beautiful Zorita," who has an unusual attachment to a boa constrictor. At the end of the trailer, we see her husband hammering a suspiciously snake-shaped lump under a rug. Jealous!

9

George Romero: On Pittsburgh Zombies and an Italian Subgenre

When he was only 15, George Romero was living the creative life. He got nailed by the police for it. It seems somebody saw him throw a body off a building.

He was growing up in New York, dreaming of the movies. His father's art studio made posters and banners for all the big-budget films. George imagined himself as a film director. He thought of how he would direct the great stories the banners announced.

That was what led to the body-tossing incident. He and his friends were shooting an 8mm film, and they wanted a realistic effect. So up to the roof they went. Never mind that their dummy was something rigged up by teenagers. It looked real enough to scare the devil out of people who saw it falling; they thought they saw somebody get thrown off a roof. Police phones started ringing.

So, Romero had to explain to the police just what he was doing tossing dummies off the roof. They told him he needed to grow up. Fortunately, for horror film fans, he never did.

It was good for a number of Italian filmmakers that he didn't, too. For Romero's *Dead* trilogy, particularly *Dawn of the Dead*, would spawn a spaghetti subgenre. Not only would Pittsburgh have zombie troubles, Italy would be overrun by them.

Before we start unleashing zombie armies to go stomping through Italy, let's see how Romero came to make his first zombie epic.

After high school, Romero decided to attend the Carnegie Institute of Technology in Pittsburgh. Here, he would meet several of the people who would later band together as a film company that would make the classic *Night of the Living Dead*. First, he would make friends with Rudy Ricci. Through Ricci, he would be introduced to John Russo, who would write the script for the zombie shocker. Later, Russell Streiner would join the group. He would coproduce the film, along with Romero, and play the part of Johnny. Remember how he taunted his sister with the line, "They're coming to get you, Barbara," just before the zombie got him?

But for now, there were no zombies for anyone to worry about. Romero spent his time going to class and drawing in his sketch pads. He honed his talents with 8mm filmmaking and wondered about life after college.

A summer's work as a gofer on the movie *Bell, Book, and Candle* persuaded Romero that he could make a feature film. All he needed to do was persuade his friends. As it turned out, they were as ready as he was. Somehow they managed to borrow $2,000 to make their film. Until then, they had been shooting mostly comedies, like takeoffs of spy movies and imitations of Peter Sellars. Now that they were doing a feature, no matter how modest, they would stick with comedy, but do things that were less derivative.

They bought a used Bolex 16mm camera and a supply of film stock. The movie would be structured like the little films they had been making. It was a collection of humorous sketches that they gathered together under the title *Expostulations*. Once the movie was finished, they were presented with a problem. What do you do with a feature-length comedy with no soundtrack? There had been no money for sync sound equipment when they started shooting. They had hoped that afterward they could dub the soundtrack, but there was just no money available.

Romero and Streiner had an idea. They already had a camera and lights. Why not go into the commercial film business? Pittsburgh was booming in those days. Industrial training films, corporate business films, and television commercials all seemed like possibilities. They could take their profits and use them on a soundtrack for *Expostulations*.

As fate would have it, they were headed down the road toward feature film success, but it would have nothing to do with the movie they had shot. Their little company was just too strapped financially to dub a soundtrack for the film. The Latent Image, their company that would later make *Night of the Living Dead*, would have a long, hard time of it.

They started out in a cheap storefront in a rough part of town. All the corporate films and television spots that they had dreamed of getting went to other companies. They got by, by shooting stills. They did baby pictures, weddings — whatever came their way, for whatever was offered. They were so poor they couldn't afford heat in the winter. Worse, they were having trouble just feeding themselves. Still, they would not quit.

Then a break came their way. The Buhl Planetarium needed a commercial and wanted to use the theme of landing on the moon, the country's goal in space exploration. The trouble was, as always, money. The planetarium had only $1,600 to spend.

The folks at the planetarium had taken their money to the right place. To Romero and Streiner, $1,600 was all the money in the world. These were guys who had made a feature film for $2,000. Why, of course, they could do a small commercial for $1,600.

Romero started painting backdrops, Streiner created a lunar surface on a tabletop, and they called in Rudy Ricci's brother to build a landing craft. Mark Ricci was a college student and model rocket enthusiast; he built sophisticated, radio-controlled rockets. The filmmakers were packing the commercial with production values, intent on making this break work for them.

As it turned out, $1,600 wasn't enough. The commercial lost money, but gained attention. Things began to look up for them. Jobs began to come their way. Low-dollar jobs, to be sure, but jobs making films. More talented people joined their company, including John Russo, just out of the army.

It is hard to say whether buying the 35mm Arriflex camera triggered their desire to make a feature, or if it was a thought that had been in their minds all along. But as soon as they got the 35mm, the talk and the planning began.

As young fellows they had tried a comedy and weren't able to finish it. What they needed was something surefire, with a built-in audience, that they could sell investors on. Horror always pulled people into the drive-ins. The quality of what was being made was rotten. They knew they could beat it.

Romero and nine others connected with the Latent Image kicked in $600 each. Even for the lowest of low-budget projects, $5,400 wouldn't get them anywhere. (They weren't in touch with Andy Milligan. He might have made a picture on that kind of budget.) Still, it was seed money. They had enough to get them started.

John Russo started writing a script about the dead coming back to life. Romero and Streiner started rounding up a cast and locations and hunted for more money. They were about to pull off a miracle.

The same sort of spirit that had held their little company together when they had no heat in their storefront and no money for lunch began to show itself as they shot the movie. One scene required a zombie to catch fire when a bomb was thrown. They had no fireproof suit and no stuntman, even if they'd had one.

Deciding he could wear more hats than scriptwriter, Russo volunteered for the job. He put on layer after layer of clothing for protection and let them torch him. It was incredibly dangerous, but he managed to come through it without getting hurt.

Their movie required 30 shooting days that were scattered over seven months. The $5,400 had evaporated almost immediately. They would shoot film as long as they had money; then when it ran out, they would hunt

Molotov cocktails make an effective weapon against zombies in *Night of the Living Dead*.

for more investors or a side job shooting a commercial to get the money to start again.

Eventually, they would put $114,000 into the film. They had many times that amount of value on the screen because so many people did more than one job. And some folks worked for free. Many of the zombie extras played their parts just for the fun of being in a movie.

Romero had his film. Now, he had to get it out to the public. He and his partners began shopping it around to the major distributors, but without much success. AIP liked it, but thought the ending was too depressing. Columbia said no because the movie was in black and white. Finally, they showed it to one of the smaller distributors, the Walter Reade Organization, which made Romero and his friends an offer, one that seemed like a good one to the inexperienced group. Though Romero and his friends would later rue the day they had signed the agreement, for the time being they were happy.

There is a legend about the initial release of *Night of the Living Dead*. It seems that the movie was mistakenly booked into a Saturday afternoon "spook show," a kiddy matinee where parents left off their children while they went shopping. When the parents came back for them, the children were scared out of their wits. The parents were outraged, and hot words were spoken.

If the parents had seen what their children had, probably more than hot words would have been exchanged. Zombie cannibals chowing down was new in 1968. Some of the scenes were the most offensive things offered outside an H. G. Lewis movie.

Yet, this movie went beyond shocking the audience. It was able to involve the viewers so much that they felt trapped in the farmhouse with Ben and Barbara and the others. *Night of the Living Dead* was one of the rare films that was able to create the feeling of a nightmare.

Word of mouth spread the news about it. People sought out the movie wherever they could, whether it was at a drive-in or an inner-city theater. People flocked to see it. Romero and his gang had a hit on their hands.

But they weren't getting any money back, or at least very little. The deal they had struck with the distributor was now showing itself to be a poor one. To make matters worse, the Walter Reade Organization was too small to have clout with theaters and subdistributors hundreds of miles away. If a theater was slow in paying or was giving a short count, there wasn't much they could do about it.

But at the least, Romero and his friends had a wonderful start in feature films. Why it took 11 more years for Romero to equal his success with his first feature film is a tale of hard luck and opportunities missed.

The Affair was his first attempt. Everyone who saw it says it was an excellent little romantic comedy. The trouble was that almost nobody saw it. The distributor they tried gave it the briefest possible release and then shelved it.

This broke up the group. Though many of them would have careers in film, Romero was now on his own.

He set up a great deal to make three movies for a film brokerage. It was too good to be true. The brokerage collapsed halfway through filming what could have been a classic, *Season of the Witch*. Romero was left holding

One of the best remembered shots from Lucio Fulci's *Zombie*.

the bag. He finished the film, borrowing money and going deeply into debt.

The Crazies was made on a considerably smaller budget than was *Season of the Witch*. Again, poor distribution would foil a good effort. Several years passed before Romero tried again.

For the modern vampire story, *Martin*, Tom Savini would come on board, starting a long, profitable association with Romero. The film would break Romero's drought at the box office. While not a breakaway hit, it did well enough to gain favorable attention from the money men, and the critics were intrigued by Romero's direction.

Romero was set for success. *Dawn of the Dead* would bring it to him, as well as worldwide recognition. This dark-humored tale takes up where *Night of the Living Dead* left off. For those who might have thought the zombies had been defeated, there was a heck of a surprise. Not only had they not been defeated, they were ready to go shopping.

Romero's famous shot of the zombies roaming back and forth in the shopping mall was both a comic highlight and a wry observation on modern surburban life. However, its superviolent effects would take many early headlines.

Savini says the effects were all done quickly, but when you watch the movie, you realize the reason for their quickness was because Savini is a

The living dead chow down in *Zombie*.

master. The favorite effect of many is when the zombie walks into the helicopter blade.

You see the zombie coming toward the helicopter. He has a strangely high forehead. You think, "Are they going to to what I think they're going to do?" Sure enough, wap! Off with the top of his head. Gorehounds never fail to cheer.

The film did good business in the United States and went through the roof in Europe. Several Italian filmmakers were quick to take notice.

Although the Italian cinema has produced much great original work, genre filmmakers in Italy had to convince backers that there was a sure market for their product. One way they were able to do so was to come up with something similar to a successful American film. Without really intending to, Romero led the Italians to a new genre: the spaghetti zombie movie.

As with the spaghetti western, these movies would win the admiration of American fans. Though for the most part they weren't as artfully done as was *Dawn of the Dead*, they made up for any shortcomings by sheer recklessness.

Take *Zombie*, for instance. In the film, there is a scene of a girl's face being pulled toward a splintered door. The splinter gets closer and closer to her eye. The tension this builds in the viewer is almost unbearable. When the camera refuses to cut away and the audience watches the splinter sink in, they are floored.

Zombie's director, Lucio Fulci, rushed the film out to take advantage of all the stir following *Dawn of the Dead*. In Italy, *Dawn* had been released under the title *Zombie*. So, Fulci called his movie *Zombie II* in Italy. It also went under the title *Zombie Flesh Eaters* in some locations.

Fulci would follow this success in the genre with *Gates of Hell*, starring Christopher George, and a graveyard full of zombies. This film insured Fulci a cult following in the United States.

Now, if you're looking for machine-gun-toting zombies and zombies getting blasted into hash by said weapons, look no further than *City of Walking Dead*. This has to be the wackiest film of the bunch. It gleefully loads on the gore, while sparking unintentional humor. My favorite moment is the shot of the zombies hanging onto the Volkswagen as it goes careening along. One of the zombies is looking forward as if to say, "Isn't this thing going a bit fast?"

Even though the film occasionally turns the zombies into cartoon figures, some moments are well done. The sequence in which the couple is pursued by zombies in the amusement park has the thrill of a good adventure movie. If you're into realistic machine-gun hits, the kind that make zombie heads burst like melons, then these scenes are for you.

10

Fred Olen Ray: The Direct-to-Video King

There are stories about filmmakers who had no money when they started, there are stories about filmmakers who had no equipment, and there are stories about filmmakers who had no cast or script. But Fred Olen Ray may be the only one who had absolutely none of the most basic ingredients needed. Except for one: an overwhelming desire to make movies.

Ray worked for a television station in Florida and was hoping to find a way to make films in his spare time. This was in the mid–1970s, a glorious time for low-budget exploitation films that made substantial amounts of money from tiny investments. But Ray saw no possible way to stir up even the small budget necessary to do a film the right way.

Now, doing a film any way at all was another matter. He decided to attack the problem in the most basic fashion.

To make a film, he needed a camera. It just happened that the television station where he worked had decided to retire one of its old workhorse cameras, an Auricon 16mm. The Auricon was an excellent instrument, used in the 1960s and 1970s before widespread use of videotape equipment in news gathering. When you watch footage from Vietnam or other events of that era, the odds are good that it was shot with an Auricon.

Ray asked if he could borrow the old camera. Not only would the people at the station let him use the camera, but there was also some old black-and-white film stock in their refrigerator that they wanted to get rid of. No one knew if it was still any good, since it had been in the refrigerator for ages, but it had been properly stored the entire time.

Ray knew that black-and-white stock was far more stable than color stock. The odds were that it was still good. It also was magnetic striped film, which meant better-quality sound. There was another important factor. The station was willing to give it to him, rather than let it go to waste.

He now had a camera and film. Finding a cast was the next problem.

Professionals were out of the question. There was no money to pay anybody. He would have to take whoever he could get.

There is something about the idea of making a movie that captivates people. Few have so little imagination that they have never fantasized about being an actor. So, there was a fair number of amateur actors, some with no experience whatsoever, to draw from.

This left the problem of getting a script. Although some people may dispute that Ray's first project, now called *The Brain Leeches*, ever had a script, Ray turned out to be a writer of considerable skill, though *The Brain Leeches* may not be the best place to look for it.

Don't take that last statement as a mean remark. Ray had somehow gotten his project this far without spending a cent. He manfully wrestled his amateur cast, aging camera, and black-and-white film stock through shooting. His only expense was to get the film developed. Since the film was black and white, this step was dirt cheap.

Ray took his footage back to the television station and transferred it to video for his final edit. He was allowed time on the machines for free, as long as he used them when nobody else needed them.

Ray has joked that *The Brain Leeches* cost $298 to make. That's a joke that's probably close to the truth. He calls it a disaster, but it is important, if to no one else but Ray. It gave him experience, allowed him to learn from his mistakes, and gave him a credit for his résumé. A very good use of $298.

For his next film, Ray wanted star power and managed to get it because of a meeting he had engineered some time before.

Ray loved the old movie serials. He had grown up at a time when many of the best had just been sold to television. All the greats, like Flash Gordon, were turning up on local television. They were a staple of afternoon and Saturday programming. Other attractions, like many of the Tarzan features, were bought and played over and over.

Buster Crabbe was their star. The roles he played in these action-packed films were vigorously athletic, which suited Crabbe well. Often he did his own stunts.

Many times you hear of Hollywood legends who were in top physical condition during their performing years and then later went to pot. Not Crabbe. He stayed in shape, competing in various athletic events.

A program called *Golden Age Olympics* was going to be filmed. Ray volunteered to be a cameraman at the event, just so he could get to meet Crabbe. Although they probably didn't discuss particular projects, an aspiring filmmaker like Ray certainly must have had something in mind.

Ray was hoping to make a better picture than *The Brain Leeches* — one that could get some serious distribution. He decided to make a short film to attract investors.

It would showcase what he believed was his best skill — special effects makeup. He made a monster mask and a pair of hands. He put them on a guy wearing bib overalls and shot him chasing a girl around in a local park.

The next thing he needed was an investor. Through an association of film industry people, Ray met a man who had worked for exploitation king Jerry Gross. This man had recently retired, but wanted to stay involved in the movie business.

Ray got out his projector and showed him the footage on the living room wall. The man was enthusiastic, but how much would it cost?

Ray guessed the total budget needed would be $15,000. The man put up $5,000 and got another backer to come in with $5,000. Now Ray had to kick in.

He got a loan by putting up his motorcycle as collateral and getting his mother to cosign the note. The $15,000 was there. It was time to line up a cast.

He wrote to Buster Crabbe, describing the project and asking him to take the part of the sheriff. If Crabbe would say yes, Ray's little monster film would have a name star and a real chance at distribution.

Since Crabbe had friends in Florida who he could visit, he said yes. It would be a kind of working vacation. He hadn't done a film in a while and really seemed to like the idea.

Ray set about filming *The Alien Dead*. Since $15,000 will only go so far, most of the other actors were local amateurs. However, his effects were as good as any seen at that time. Mostly he stayed with basic gore effects, like a pitchfork through a torso. He even used the monster in overalls scene that attracted the investors, taking the same footage and fitting it right in.

Surprising for the extreme low budget were a few brief nude and seminude shots. Ray couldn't resist combining a traditional skinny-dipping scene with having the monster go after the pretty girl.

In most Hollywood movies, you couldn't shoot the scene just mentioned for under $15,000. Ray managed to shoot his entire movie for less. It only cost him $12,000 to complete *The Alien Dead*.

Even though he made an excellent little film, it was four years before Ray got a chance to direct again. When the opportunity came, it was for the movie *Scalps* (1982).

He stuck to the low-budget gore genre, the difference this time being that he had a little more money and a professional cast, though all were unknowns. Trying to put all his small budget on the screen, he cut corners everywhere else. Rather than provide transportation, everyone drove his or her car to the day's location. Often this meant a small community out in the desert. Since there was no money for things like caterers, they would make sandwiches. Nor was there money for niceties like trailers for dressing rooms or even rest rooms. To dodge this problem, they made friends

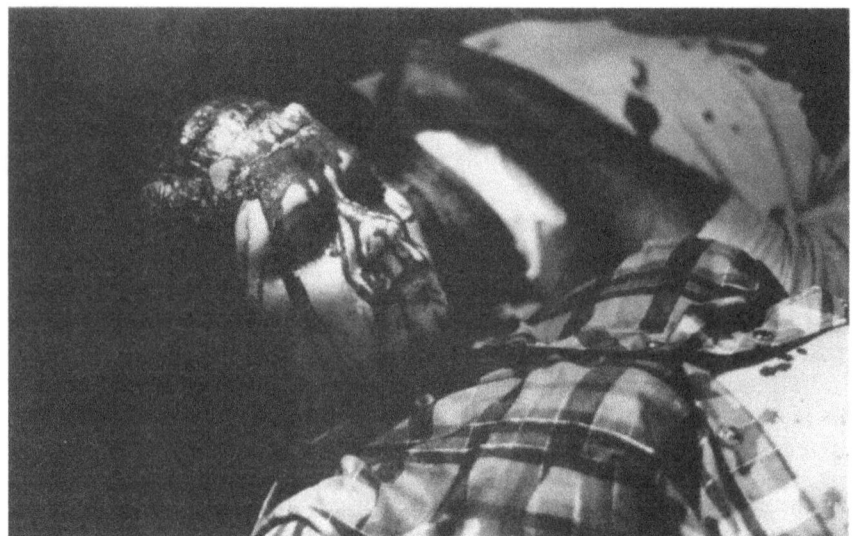

Picked as Dog of the Week by Siskel and Ebert, *Scalps* went on to drive-in success.

with people who owned homes nearby. No one was left hunting for a clump of bushes if he or she didn't want to, though the nearest house might be a long walk away.

The worst problem with making a low-budget film on location isn't the lack of a rest room or the quality of the peanut butter used in the sandwiches. It's the lack of basic technical services that most filmmakers take for granted. For Ray, it was getting his dailies back on time.

When most of us think of dailies, or rushes, as some people call them, we think of actors watching a scene they appeared in the day before. It seems to be a tool used to appraise and improve their performance. Of course, it is that. It is also much more.

Dailies are needed to spot the most basic problems. Often if something is wrong with a camera, it goes unnoticed until the next day when you look at your dailies. This was exactly what happened to Ray. A camera was malfunctioning, spoiling his footage.

If he had found out the day after the problem began, it wouldn't have been so bad. But he was using an out-of-town lab. The lab wasn't sending dailies. It wasn't even sending weeklies. One batch of film took three weeks to get back.

Hundreds of feet of film were spoiled by the defective camera. Ray was left trying to piece together a film out of what he had. It wasn't a matter of selecting the best shot, but of trying to find usable footage. In a few cases he was able to reshoot, but not nearly as much as he would have liked.

One scene the distributor forced him to reshoot, though he didn't want to. In the movie there is a rape scene. In its original version, the scene was shot without nudity because Ray thought that it shouldn't be presented in a way that was overly graphic.

The people at the distribution company thought otherwise. They demanded that nudity be added, and if Ray wouldn't do it, they would. To prevent the mangling of his film, Ray reshot the scene. He has remained disturbed about it ever since.

In spite of the film's disappointments for Ray, it was his first chance at widespread notoriety. The notice was provided by Ebert and Siskel, on their old PBS show. *Scalps* was given their Dog of the Week award.

This bit of negative publicity put gorehounds everywhere on alert. They rushed out to see it, putting *Scalps* on Variety's list of top 50 grossing movies.

Ray was now at the point in his career when he could look for projects that were a step beyond the ultra low-budget affairs he had directed up to now. But with deal making being what it is in Hollywood, it was two more years until he made his next real success, *Biohazard*, on which he served as director, producer, and screenwriter. And it would be two more years, almost a decade after he made *The Brain Leeches*, that he would make his breakaway video hit *The Tomb*. Almost overnight *The Tomb* sold 40,000 copies for its distributor, Transworld, which made a fortune from cassette sales and the television rights.

In agreeing to do the project for Transworld, Ray gave up the right to the final cut of the picture. Although much is made of having the right to say exactly what goes in the print the public sees, in reality, few directors have this privilege.

In the theatrical version that Ray controlled, there was a fair amount of sex and violence. Ray didn't include these elements needlessly. There were important pieces of plotting tied up in these scenes.

Transworld, fearing it might have problems selling the movie in foreign markets, made hash of the video. Much of the black humor, which was becoming one of Ray's trademarks, was tied up in some of the more violent sequences. And almost all of it was removed. Gore, by now, was getting a bad name in the marketplace because of the censorship groups around the world.

Most regrettable to girl watchers were the cuts made in the television print. Michelle Bauer's nude scenes were cut, as was Kitten Natividad's entire part. You can't help but think of Transworld as a bunch of spoilsports.

From the success of *The Tomb* onward, Ray has made a continuous string of hits. An audience favorite was the comedy-horror film *Hollywood Chainsaw Hookers*.

Sold with the slogan "they'll cost you an arm and a leg," this wildly funny and inventive movie featured Ray regular Michelle Bauer as one of the chainsaw-toting hookers. She has what must be one of the film's most memorable scenes.

In the scene, she takes a "date" back to her room and tells him to lie down and close his eyes. As he lies there, eyes clenched shut, she takes off her clothes. It looks like the beginning of a sex scene. Then, strangely, she starts to cover everything in the room with sheets of plastic, including her Elvis poster. She even puts on a shower cap.

Then Bauer speaks. "Now, I'm going to send you to heaven."

Her date lies there, his eyes still closed, squirming with anticipation. "Yeah baby," he says. "Send me to heaven."

So she whips out her saw, and sends him to heaven.

Only a few minutes into the movie, the audience already had its money's worth. Imagine the glee of first-time viewers when they discover who the ringleader of this bloodthirsty gang is. It's none other than Leatherface himself, Gunnar Hansen. This hero to chainsaw fanciers everywhere plays the leader of a cult who use chainsaws as a part of their weird religious rites.

While Ray had censorship problems with *The Tomb*, in Britain even the title of *Hollywood Chainsaw Hookers* was censored. The words *Hollywood*, and *hookers*, well, they were all right, but *chainsaw?* Now that was going too far. Combining three words like that in the same title, why, it might bring the country to its knees. So the word *chainsaw* had to go.

The film's British distributor figured a crafty way around that problem. He printed the words *Hollywood* and *hookers* and placed a picture of a chainsaw between them. Sure that all the proprieties were being observed, the censors allowed this title to pass.

Among Ray's latest films is *The Phantom Empire*, the story about explorers in search of a lost city. What the explorers find is the biggest assortment of secondhand movie props around, including the barbeque spit from *History of the World, Part 1*.

11

Super 8: The New Medium of Choice

Many of the filmmakers in this book made their films on 35mm or 16mm, when the money wasn't there for 35mm. In general terms, film stock and equipment are the smallest items on a movie's budget. But when you make the kind of movie I've been talking about, for which the budget is whatever the director can sell his car for, it's a different matter. Paying $30 to $40 for two and a half minutes of film stock and processing (the workprint is extra) for 16mm can eat up a pocket-change budget fast.

It did not used to be that way; 35mm was reasonable, and 16mm was dirt cheap. Amateurs used it in their wind-up Bolexes and Bell and Howells. Then greed entered the equation, in the form of the Hunt brothers.

The Hunt brothers had no thought of film stock when they hatched their plan. What they wanted to do was corner the market on silver futures. If people like the Hunt brothers have a spare billion or so lying around, they can amuse themselves with such little tricks.

The Hunt brothers came close to pulling off their stunt. In doing so they drove the price of silver futures, and of silver itself, sky high. The average person sat back and marveled at the goings on, and perhaps got a wry chuckle when the Hunts' plan fell apart, costing them and fellow suckers an untold amount of money.

But for filmmakers, the whole thing had been a disaster. Silver salts are the more important part of film stock production. Since their price had risen with the market, Kodak and other manufacturers had to raise the price of film. When silver prices tumbled, crunching the Hunt brothers beneath them, film prices stayed high. Kodak and the rest cited the many years that prices had gone unchanged, while they had spent millions on research and development. There would be no more cheap film.

Independents were stuck. Some of them had seen the wisdom of owning the means of production—the cameras, editing benches, and the like. Those who owned 35mm equipment were astounded to discover that film prices had more than doubled overnight. If they were to shoot with their gear, every corner had to be cut. They would be forced to shoot less film, often having to make do with a shot that wasn't quite good enough, thus degrading a product that might be on shaky ground to start with.

Sometimes, making do with less wasn't enough. The search for thrift led some low-budget producers to try something they hadn't done since their amateur days. They shot "short ends"—unused, leftover portions of rolls of film that big-timers break off and return to the lab when they don't need to use an entire roll. The trouble with short ends is that you don't know if they are any good when you get them. They may well be fogged, and the only way you can find out for sure is to shoot a test strip with each roll. It's time consuming, but if you don't, the result may be disaster. And you can forget about getting all the film from the same batch, so that the colors match perfectly. You just take what you can get and hope for the best.

To a lot of people, this all meant that 16mm was the route to take. While 16mm's price had jumped, it was still cheaper than 35mm. But this was only true to those who looked at the surface of the problem. Underneath, it was a different matter.

Because 35mm is the required gauge for projection in the world's theaters, if you're going to shoot a film in 16mm, you still have to blow it up to 35mm. At that time, the price of a blowup was $15,000 to $20,000 for a good-quality job. That price effectively blew the savings of shooting in 16mm.

Though many people didn't realize it, the answer to their problems was lying at hand. A few brave souls were already trying it. Some were already making a profit.

When you think of movies shot in the Philippines, you probably think of Roger Corman's women-in-cages films or John Ashley's bamboo girl movies. You don't think of native product. As a matter of fact, much of the Filipino film industry has been aimed toward supplying outside movie crews with equipment and services. There have been Filipino movies, shot in the Tagalog dialect, but they have had limited success.

Narcisco and Domingo Arong had nothing to do with the Filipino film industry. Actually, neither of them had ever held a movie camera before. They didn't know an f-stop from a shortstop. So why did they decide to get into the movie business?

They were successful businessmen, owning a company that exported puka shells to the United States—two brothers, both young, who were making a mark for themselves. But just how exciting is a puka shell? Do puka shell exporters have fans? Is there any glamour involved in it? For that matter, just how creative can you get with these things? One suspects the answer to these questions is "not much." The movies beckoned.

The Arong brothers had a tailor-made opportunity lying at hand, ready to be exploited. Though most movies made in the Philippines for Filipino audiences are made in the Tagalog dialect, the central and southern parts of the country dislike the language. They prefer Cebuano, and all the top radio shows for the area are done in it.

Going to the movies in the south or central Philippines is a somewhat disagreeable experience for the locals because Tagalog is a difficult language for them to follow. But they either saw these movies or did not go because all movies produced in Manila were in Tagalog.

The Arong brothers reasoned that a film shot in Cebuano would take in some bucks at the box office. It would have to have lots of action because that was what the audience wanted. It would have to be in color, bright color, because they lived in a tropical country. And it would have to be about something that everybody in the area liked.

There was a radio program about a man named Esteban, a poor fellow who was a gamecock fighter, and the adventures he had. If they could get the rights to the program, the Arong brothers would have two angles going for them: It was a popular show and it was about the country's most popular sport.

Getting the rights wasn't hard. Who wanted to make a movie in Cebuano? Nobody in Manila, and Manila controlled the film industry.

Controlled isn't a strong-enough word. Had a stranglehold may be more accurate. If you wanted to do a movie in Manila, you did it with the industry's cameras and film stock — and at its prices. The Arong brothers knew that working with the Manila industry would eat up their profits if they tried to do things the traditional way.

Still, they had the rights to the show. Domingo started to work on a script, even though the brothers had no idea how they would shoot it. These guys really had a positive mental attitude. Narciso had to keep the puka shell business going, so he took a plane to the United States to check on things at that end.

He made inquiries of everyone who might know anything about filmmaking, without much luck. Then, one day at a newsstand, he saw a copy of *Super 8 Filmmaker Magazine.* He looked it over and thought this medium had possibilities. He sent the copy home to his brother.

Domingo dug into it. This was the answer. It was a simple system: lightweight, which meant it would be great for filming action, and best of all, the Manila film industry had no say over it. It was considered an amateur medium, of no value to the professionals. The government didn't even tax it when it came into the country, the way it did 16mm and 35mm.

Domingo sent back for more issues of this magazine. He studied them and decided what he needed. He told Narciso to get a Kodak XL and have it modified to run at 24fps. They would also need a Canon 1014, one of the best Super 8 cameras ever made. To capture their precious Cebuano dialogue, they would need a Super 8 Sound fullcoat recorder.

Narcisco faithfully rounded up all this gear and shipped it to the Philippines. Along with it, he sent 120 cartridges of Ektachrome film and 10,000 feet of fullcoat magnetic tape for the recorder. They had everything they needed to shoot their feature.

Now, some avant garde types in the United States had shot some long Super 8 projects, and there were festivals here that featured only Super 8 work, but a commercial feature was another matter. Super 8 might pop up on television news, if say, someone caught sight of a tornado with a movie camera. But in the Philippines, Super 8 was just something tourists pointed at you. When the boys in Manila heard what Domingo was up to, they laughed. It was impossible to make it work.

The Arong brothers refused to be discouraged. Domingo got the cast of the radio show to play their roles in the film. The cast didn't think much of their chances with the tiny cameras and the first-time director, so they did it cheap. No use to soak the poor guys. Besides, making a movie, any kind of movie, might be fun.

Domingo still needed men to operate the recorder, to handle the mike boom, and gaffers. There were a lot of guys working in the puka shell factory. He pulled them out of the factory and made himself a crew. Nobody knew how to do anything. That was okay because Domingo didn't know either. He was reading the instruction manuals, staying about one step ahead of the fellows he was trying to train. Finally, they were ready to start shooting.

The film's name was to be *Manok Ni San Pedro* or, in English, *The Gamecock of St. Peter*. Saint Peter is considered to be the patron saint of cockfighting, at least by the Filipinos. Esteban, the lead character, was to see old St. Peter twice during the course of this wildly plotted adventure.

Esteban may have been poor, but he had won the heart of his boss's daughter, the fair Liza. Too bad that Liza was promised to the evil Don Miguel, who happened to be rich and powerful. Don Miguel couldn't stand knowing that Liza preferred Esteban.

In a scene worthy of "Sea Hunt," Don Miguel has his goons attack Esteban while Esteban is scuba diving. The goons cut Esteban's air hose and leave him to die. Sure enough, the next stop is the pearly gates, and the first encounter with St. Peter.

St. Peter greets Esteban warmly, but tells him he will have to go back to Earth; his time hasn't come yet. Far from being relieved, Esteban is depressed. Life for him had been a series of disappointments. Why would he want to go back to all that misery, when heaven beckoned.

St. Peter gives him a fighting cock. This is no ordinary bird. Not only will it win every fight it is entered in, it can talk. Esteban goes back to Earth with his prize.

Don Miguel, obsessed sleaze that he is, challenges Esteban to a cockfight, with the winner to have the hand of Liza. Esteban goes for it, seeing now why St. Peter gave him the bird. But Don Miguel is no fool. His thugs steal the magic bird and replace it with a lookalike that was the Jean Pierre Coopman of roosters. (Muhammad Ali clobbered Coopman in a title defense that took fewer than four rounds.)

Don Miguel might be able to have a rooster switched, but it doesn't pay to mess around with St. Peter. St. Peter intended Esteban's rooster to win, and it would. The bird pulled a Rocky Balboa and won.

Don Miguel is not the sort of fellow to take such things gracefully. He kidnaps Liza and heads for the airport.

Esteban races after them on a motorcycle. Now he turns into Bruce Lee, kicking and chopping Don Miguel's goons left and right. Soon, no one is left standing between Esteban and Don Miguel.

Don Miguel proves himself a coward. He pulls out a gun and shoots Esteban. Liza runs to the fallen Esteban, while Don Miguel escapes in his plane.

Esteban is taking a trip, too. Back to the pearly gates and St. Peter. This Esteban really has a thing for near-death experiences. St. Peter tells him to go back; it's still not his time. Then Esteban sees who is in back of him in line. It's Don Miguel. He had a bit of trouble with his plane and crashed it. Too bad.

Like they said, the Arong brothers wanted a movie with lots of action. It took six weeks to shoot. Super 8 was turning out to be a real plus for them, instead of just a way to get their film made. They could get their film developed right in the Philippines and have it back within two days, which was almost as good as getting rushes. And it cost only a fraction of what it would have cost in 16mm. They even shot underwater scenes with the Kodak, using an underwater housing that Narcisco sent over.

With the film in the can, Domingo was ready to start editing. Narcisco went back to Super 8 Sound, this time buying an editing bench, and sending it home.

There was Domingo, with all that footage and all that sound track, and no idea how to synchronize it. He tried to synchronize it, but either the actors' mouths moved and no voices came out or the voices came out of the wrong mouths. Finally, he found a book, *The Handbook of Super 8 Production*, and started picking his way out of the mess.

To get the completed movie into theaters, the Arong brothers would have to get it blown up to 35mm. While 16mm was commonly being blown up to 35mm, Super 8 was another matter. Here, they had the good luck to find a master. Michael Hinton, of Interformat, not only had experience, he was producing blowups that rivaled 35mm in quality. He took their film and gave them something they would be proud to screen.

Manok Ni San Pedro was wildly successful. Though the average cost of a ticket in the theaters it played was less than 40 cents, it grossed over $250,000. It had cost the brothers less than $25,000 to produce—including the blowup.

It seemed for a while that this might be the road for American filmmakers to travel. Hundreds of multiplex theaters were opening. With all those screens available, the way seemed open for a renaissance of filmmaking. There would be something for everybody, and endless opportunities for the filmmakers.

Well, we saw how that turned out. Instead of a theater with eight screens playing eight different movies, we wound up with eight screens covered with the same Hollywood slop on every one. Never mind that the titles are different, they're all the same high-gloss, no-heart films.

But another revolution was getting started at about the same time. The VCR was changing people's viewing habits in a way that had never been anticipated. All those people who wanted to see something different, when they wanted to see it, could do so now. Video stores started to open—first just in the big cities, then in the small towns, and finally on every streetcorner. And all of them needed tapes to rent.

In the beginning, you could rent *The Sound of Music* or a porno tape. That was about all that was available. Then producers began to see the potential of the market and suddenly, a VCR was really worth having.

With every tape that came out almost automatically selling in the tens of thousands, people began to investigate the chances of making movies specifically for this market. Some tried, shooting videotape instead of film, and most failed. The things looked like soap operas. The richness of film was lost.

Others tried low-budget 16mm and even 35mm projects, the idea being to make back the cost of the film on the cassette sales and go into profit by selling the foreign rights. This strategy worked. The trouble was, the filmmaker would have to raise $100,000 or more to get the job done.

Since VCRs had come out, people had been trying to transfer their home movies to videotape, so they could have the convenience of watching them on television. The results were surprisingly good. Fotomat and other companies began to offer the service. A notion was born in people's minds.

Super 8 footage that was shot carefully, with professional standards of lighting and contrast, looked indistinguishable from 16mm when transferred to tape. And Super 8 film stock cost only about a third of what 16mm did. It was time for some brave soul to jump in and give it a try.

Mark Pirro was and is one of those people for whom there is no other choice in life but to make films. He was going to do it no matter what the obstacles were. That he had no way of getting into the Hollywood system didn't bother him. That he had no money to finance a film himself didn't

Pirro and Marya Gant in *A Polish Vampire in Burbank.*

turn him away. Because what he did have outweighed anything that stood in his way. He had an open mind, a sense of humor, and the initiative to do something with them.

Pirro had been making films in Super 8 for years. He knew what the medium was capable of. If he was going to get the chance to make a feature, he would have to do it in Super 8 because there was no genie around to give him $100,000.

Left: **The vampire's castle was shot as a miniature for** *A Polish Vampire in Burbank.* *Right:* **Note the homemade camera blimp Pirro used for sound takes.**

In 1985, he started work on *A Polish Vampire in Burbank*. His budget was whatever he happened to have in his pocket on the day he was filming, though he did make sure to keep track of all his expenses. By the time he was done, he had spent the grand sum of $2,500.

Most people's reaction to that ridiculously low figure is that he must have made an awful picture. The exact opposite is true. Horror-comedies are difficult to make. The chance to offend one part of the audience or another is great. Just making people laugh is tough enough.

Pirro's spoof of the vampire genre is filled with laughs. His story concerns a young vampire with a problem: He doesn't want to bite people. When he finally finds a young lady to chow down on, he falls in love with her instead.

In almost every vampire movie there is a "race the dawn" sequence, in which the vampire must hurry to make it back to his coffin before the sun comes up. The one Pirro has in this film is hilarious. Not since the days of silent movies has there been such a wildly funny slapstick scene.

Pirro acted in the film, playing the part of the young vampire. He shows considerable talent, winning the audience's sympathy. As a whole, the cast was excellent. You can only wonder how he found such talented people to work for him, when he had no money to spend.

Poster for *Curse of the Queerwolf.*

For his hard work and his $2,500 investment, Pirro had a film that would gross $500,000 in cassette sales. It would also appear on national cable, on the USA network.

Pirro would follow up his success with a 35mm feature, *Death Row Gameshow.* He would return to Super 8, using an idea from his first film for *Curse of the Queerwolf.*

Three guys you don't want to meet on a walk in the woods. From *Curse of the Queerwolf*.

Pirro was soon joined by others who chose the Super 8 to video route for getting their projects done. Roger Evans had a tad more money, but not much more. The total budget for his *Jet Benny* was just $6,000. With this amount, he would produce an affectionate tribute to Jack Benny and Benny's television show.

The idea was this: What if Jack Benny had spoofed *Star Wars*? Evans supplies us with the answer. Jack would become Jet Benny, Rochester

Pirro lenses a Queerbilly for *Curse of the Queerwolf*.

would be an android, and their spaceship would be a Maxwell. This video should be seen not only by fans of Jack Benny, but by fans of 1950s television as well.

Evans's project grossed $130,000 in sales and got him a job directing *Forever Evil* for United Entertainment. This 16mm film grossed over $1 million in its first 90 days on video.

As people approach their 40th birthday, they often become reflective. They see what they've done in life, and what they haven't done. Some decide to make a change. They go on a diet or take up tennis. Others are more adventurous hairy. At age 39, Kirk Alex decided to make a movie.

This was a tall order for a Los Angeles cabbie with exactly zero beans in his pocket. But when you have to make a movie, you have to make a movie. So, he said farewell to his cab, selling it to raise the money for film stock and props.

There was no need to include any money in the budget for locations or permits. He just wasn't going to pay for those things. This was going to be hit-and-run filmmaking all the way: jump out of the truck, get the shot, then jump back in and take off. No need to tell anybody; what they didn't know wouldn't hurt them.

Alex had to do it that way. Doing it within the system would require such things as having a ranger on the set when he shot the wilderness

A musical Queerbilly takes to the trees.

scenes, for a cost of $100 per day. There would be endless paperwork, fees to pay, and bureaucrats to deal with. Guerrilla filmmaking was the way to go.

For a movie like *Lunchmeat*, it seems appropriate. This tale of a backwoods clan who murder people and then sell the flesh to barbeque stands needed to be made on the run. Having actors keep one eye peeled for the law all the time can add a little extra tension to the performance.

They did get caught. More than once. But Alex was a smooth talker and a sharp thinker. Whenever the law showed up, he would be profuse in his apologies, feigning ignorance of the rules. He would promise not to do anymore filmmaking there until he had the right permits.

He was as good as his word. He wouldn't do anymore filmmaking at that spot. He'd drive down the road a little way before he set up again. That was how he was able to get his film in the can.

It took 14 days, scattered over three months. Sometimes he stopped because of schedule conflicts for his cast members. Sometimes he stopped because there was no money for film. But he didn't quit.

Despite the hardships, *Lunchmeat* is an effective film, at times viciously so. Though it frequently puts the viewer in mind of *The Texas Chainsaw Massacre*, it also pays homage to H. G. Lewis's *Two Thousand Maniacs*. Alex even used detour signs to send his victims off the main road, the way Lewis did in *Maniacs*.

Lunchmeat was picked up by Tapeworm Video and is reportedly its best-selling tape.

Phil Vigeant, president of Super 8 Sound, says that at least 30 features were made on Super 8 in 1988. The number would be triple that in 1990.

Vigeant is the man to know such things. His Burbank, California, company sells more professional-quality Super 8 gear than anyplace else in the country. If you want to learn about Super 8, it teaches courses on both coasts of the United States. If you prefer to learn through books and manuals, it sells them. In the past, the company has even scheduled blocks of time on the Rank-Cintel flying spot scanner, so low-budget producers could get their movies transferred at "group rates." The Rank-Cintel is the most sophisticated means of transferring film to video and produces the highest-quality results.

12

Tobe Hooper: The Texas Chainsaw Massacre

For most of this book, I've refrained from writing in the first person. My feeling was that you paid your money for information, not egotism or opinions. But there are some films that make a fellow speak from the heart. The kind that moved you, the kind that made a difference in your life. For me, a formative experience as a writer and sometime filmmaker was the first time I saw *The Texas Chainsaw Massacre.*

When I say it moved me, I don't mean that I cheered on Leatherface and his saw. On the contrary, I saw it for the first time at the very place God intended for such films to be seen — at the Swan Drive-In in Blue Ridge, Georgia — and I did not cheer. As a matter of fact, if some prankster had cranked a saw in that place, I would have driven right through the screen. I was terrified. Considering the number of drivers with deer rifles hung in the back of their pickups, there could have been a tragedy. I'll guarantee you, those boys were ready to open up at the first offer.

The influence this movie had on me is hard to explain. At the time I went to see it, I had been writing a screenplay. The next morning, I tossed it in the trash. *Chainsaw* exposed it for the dreary thing it was. But I was not depressed. *Chainsaw* was filmmaking of a kind I had never seen before. That evening at the drive-in had been a learning experience of the first magnitude.

You don't learn about horror films in a school. You usually don't learn about it from your friends, unless they have a tidbit of information to toss your way. You learn about it the hard way, lumping about in decrepit theaters, buying overpriced paperbacks that you can't stand to read past the tenth page, and every now and then finding some little nugget to store away and savor.

I had been staggering around in just such a fashion for years. Yet, even before that time, it seemed that *Chainsaw* was with me.

Let me explain something. There was a time when I didn't believe in violence in films. Though it seems preposterous for a person writing a book like this to say so, I thought it was pandering. Well, of course, some violence might be necessary. I had been exposed to *Psycho* and was unnerved by it. But that was Hitchcock. He was an artist. These low-budget horror films weren't worthy of consideration.

It was at about this stage in life that I heard a commercial on the radio one day. I was driving along, listening to a rock station coming from Chattanooga. In those days, Chattanooga was heaven for a drive-in lover. Drive-ins — of all kinds and sizes, from cozy little places with house-size screens to behemoths the size of a mountain on lots that stretched out forever — were scattered all around the town. The commercial was for one of the biggest. A movie fan, I paid close attention to it.

The commercial started with the roar of a chainsaw. Then a voice said: "Who will survive, and what will be left of them? *The Texas Chainsaw Massacre*. Also: Enter the mind of the psychosexual. See *Torso*."

I looked down at the radio. Was there no limit to how low people would stoop? Cutting people up with chainsaws? Psychosexual? They'd put anything on a movie screen to try and drag people in.

Now I laugh at myself. If I were to hear such a commercial on the radio today, I'd think, "Wow, what a great double feature!" Why, I'd have to see it, even if the drive-in were in Nome, Alaska.

But I wasn't like that then. Oh, I had my moments of wondering. Like as a youngster, every year or so a movie would come to the Swan, and all the kids wanted to see it, but their parents wisely kept them at home. This was the legendary *Blood Feast*, a part of the 1960s South as strongly remembered as any part of that remarkable decade.

And there were the motorcycle movies. One of my friends got to see these films regularly and would come to school with in-depth reports. His best story was one we could hardly believe, about a biker getting his head cut off with piano wire. Years later, I would realize he had been talking about *She Devils on Wheels*, another H. G. Lewis picture.

But all this longing to taste forbidden fruit was nothing more than a child's curiosity. That, and the desire to say, "I've seen it," when talk rolled around to *Hell's Angels '69*. It would have gained me immense capital with my friends.

Certainly, none of it warped me. I grew up to be a disgustingly clean-minded person. Like I said, When I heard that commercial, I was appalled. So what was it that led me astray?

I got it in mind that I wanted to make films. And like every other yahoo who comes along, I thought making a horror movie would be easy. My idea of a horror movie was somewhere between bug-eyed monsters and loonies running around in the shadows, jumping out on people.

Realizing that I didn't have a clue as to what I was doing, I became hungry for information, going after it in any way I could. I bought magazines, read books, caught snatches of things mentioned on television. There were movies to see late at night. There were double features to catch. I was turning into a horror fan.

The more I read, the more I hunted, I kept running into that title, *The Texas Chainsaw Massacre*. It stirred memories of a television documentary, now also a legend, called *Violence in America*, broadcast on NBC, which included a clip of Leatherface chasing Sally through the brush. On the black-and-white television I watched it on, it looked like the filmmakers had shot the scene with a flashlight.

Since this was several years ago, and the program was broadcast only once because of its three-hour length, I can't be certain about all the details. But if I remember correctly, it showed part of an interview with Tobe Hooper and Kim Henkel. Here were these two gonzo hippie types with Texas accents who had made a movie — one that looked like it was shot with a flashlight. I remember thinking, so what? (How many times in the years since then have I longed to see that program. How many times have I asked people "Did you see it?" and then have gone into a long description of the documentary. I have found only two people who remember it.)

I was thoroughly tantalized by these scraps of information. On the one hand, *Chainsaw* didn't seem like much. It was a low-budget film of the kind the Medved brothers had ripped in their Golden Turkey books. No sane person who I knew of even claimed to have seen it. And the one clip I saw looked extremely crude.

But on the other hand, why was there so much smoke if there wasn't any fire? That title, the very idea of someone getting carved up with a chainsaw, made my skin crawl.

Then one day, as I passed the magazine stand in a discount store, a strange title caught my eye: *Fangoria*. There was a picture of someone's head in a refrigerator. It was the most repellent thing I had ever seen. I looked about to make sure no one was watching and went over to pick it up.

In the upper-right-hand corner was a name that made my heart race: Tobe Hooper! Maybe I was going to get some real information now.

I looked through the magazine until I found the article. Finally, some real facts. There was even a picture of Leatherface and his saw. This was one magazine I had to have.

The copy was in rough shape. It seemed that everybody had been thumbing through it. I looked about for another copy, but this was the last one. I took it over to the counter.

The lady looked at it as if I had handed her a bomb. She looked at me as if I were an axe murderer. This is something I've grown accustomed to over the years, but then it was new. I paid her and walked away with my tail between my legs.

But, by golly, I had it. I must have read that article a dozen times. It told me a lot about Hooper and about *Chainsaw*. But there was one important thing it left out: How was I ever going to get to see it?

At that time, I knew nothing about the long legal wrangle that *Chainsaw* had been going through. All I knew was that it had disappeared from general release. It seems, though, that a great many other people were curious about the film. The country was in a horror boom, and *Chainsaw* was a lost idol.

When there is money to be made, legal problems can be solved. Soon, *Chainsaw* was out on the road. I waited for it feverishly.

Then, it came to the Swan, and I had the scare of my life. You see, part of me still had that "shot with a flashlight" illusion. I just couldn't believe that it was going to be any good. That was my misfortune.

As I drove away afterward, I was convinced that the guys who made that film ought to be in jail. They ought to be locked up somewhere. The rest of the night was a sleepless one.

Through the next day, I thought about what made the film work so well. As I did, I realized what a learning experience it had been. I also realized that I was more hungry than ever for information about Hooper and *Chainsaw*. Here is what I've learned since then.

Hooper came by his Texas locale for *Chainsaw* naturally. He was born there in 1946, in Austin. *Chainsaw* would be filmed at various locations a few miles from town.

Hooper came to know Texas and several other parts of the South. His family owned hotels throughout the region, living in whichever hotel seemed to need them the most at the time. Hooper grew up in the hotels and would make his first film in a hotel basement.

He got an 8mm camera when he was ten years old and started trying to imitate the horror films of the day. Hammer's and Corman's films all were remade by the youthful Hooper, down in his basement dungeon.

He happened to grow up at one of the luckiest periods to be a filmmaker. In the flush times of the Johnson administration all kinds of grants were being given to artists and filmmakers. Hooper started a commercial film studio and made films for PBS.

During this time, he made a short subject called *The Heisters*. It was shot in the now-forgotten wide-screen format called Techniscope. Unfortunately, Hooper could find no market for his little film. Theaters were already giving up on the short. It remains virtually unseen to this day.

A documentary on the singing group Peter, Paul, and Mary became something of a breakthrough for Hooper. That is, if he had decided to continue in that direction. The temperamental stars didn't make life easy for him. He was almost fired at one point. They required him to do an extensive reedit of the film, shifting its focus from the liberal issues they originally wanted to feature and putting the group in the spotlight.

Hooper wanted to do features. Why he didn't try horror at this point is anybody's guess. These were political times, and just about everybody with a movie camera wanted to have a say. Hooper had his with films like *Eggshells*.

A film about the end of the peace movement, Hooper shot *Eggshells* on 16mm and blew it up to 35mm for release. Artistically successful, it was a dud financially. Never properly distributed, it lost the $40,000 it cost to make.

Such experiences caused him to take a cold, hard, look at the marketplace. Many stories are told about how he came by the idea for *Chainsaw*. Some say it was a sudden inspiration. Others would have it that it was a calculated plan, built around places he knew of in Texas and the story of a real-life psychopath.

The sudden-inspiration story goes like this: Hooper was out Christmas shopping. The crowds were awful. There were so many people, they were literally shoving him along with them. To get out of the crush, he dodged into a side isle.

In front of him was a display of power tools. A macabre thought of how to make the crowd scatter occurred to him. Suddenly, he realized this was his movie idea.

The trouble with this story is that years later, when *Texas Chainsaw Massacre, Part Two* came out, so did this story — except that in this version, L. M. "Kit" Carson, the movie's screenwriter, was the one doing the Christmas shopping. Which isn't to say there's nothing to the tale. Often these accounts have a kernel of truth to them.

Of course, the real-life psychopath the film may have taken inspiration from was Ed Gein. Gein lived in an area of Wisconsin off the main highway, just like the one in Texas where the murderous clan in *Chainsaw* lived. There were many other parallels. Gein fashioned pieces of his victims' skin into garments of a sort, like Leatherface did his masks. Gein liked to raid graveyards, such as the Hitchhiker did at the beginning of the film.

But the parallels are only of a superficial sort. In creating a screenplay, Hooper and Kim Henkel used Gein's crimes only as a jumping-off point. Gein's bizarre acts were sexually motivated. He exhumed corpses to obtain female body parts for his "experiments." Gein's attachment to his mother was so strong that he wanted to be like her — exactly like her. He contemplated a sex-change operation while he committed his perversions.

Chainsaw's family has no such problem with sex. All they are interested in is meat. Also, by the number of cars hidden on their property, murder must be a commonplace event for them, if all their passengers went the way of Franklin and his friends. Gein, as far as we know, only murdered two people, and the last time was his undoing. (It should be noted that a lot of woods and fields were available to Gein, and his work as a part-time handyman gave him all the free time he would have needed to hide the bodies of unknown victims in such a way that they would never be found.)

Too little has been heard about Kim Henkel, the scriptwriter, and his input. I would think it was considerable. Did he and Hooper write the script together, or did they have brainstorming sessions, after which Henkel would go away and write? Or did Hooper tell him his idea and let Henkel run with it? I've never been able to find out.

Hooper had been aiming for *Chainsaw* for quite a while before he was able to start making it. At least a year earlier, he had been searching for special actors to fit the needs of this most unusual film.

He was involved in a movie called *The Windsplitter*. Hooper, thought of by most people as a reclusive sort, was acting in the film. The story was about a free-spirited Texas youth who is run out of his hometown and goes to Hollywood and strikes it rich. But when he comes home, a band of thugs are waiting for him. Hooper was one of the thugs.

Though the quality of the cast varied, one fellow was special. He played the father of the young man. Hooper talked to him about an idea he had for a knockdown, drag out horror film he wanted to make. The fellow was Jim Siedow. Hooper already knew he wanted him for the part of the cook.

For Hooper, there was no doubt he would make the film. How he would make it, the way it would be shot, and the props he would have would depend on how big a budget could be raised. Hooper and Henkel devised different strategies to fit different possible budgets. The worst-case scenario was for a budget smaller than the one *Eggshells* had. Considerably smaller. It would have covered the necessities like film stock and would have had everybody working on speculation.

As to the actual budget that was raised, three amounts are commonly given. One account has it at $90,000; another, at $110,000; and the highest, at $155,000. Whichever it was, it wasn't much as movies go.

Now that they had their budget together, it was time to go out and find some more actors. Hooper decided that the ideal place to look was the University of Texas in Austin.

They set up shop there and began an informal series of auditions. Word quickly spread among the drama students. Ed Neal, who would become a cult figure in his role as the hitchhiker, was hanging out with some other students when they got the news.

Just for the sake of checking it out, they decided to go over. Who made movies in Texas, anyway? They took it all as a kind of joke. Beforehand, they had been told that the movie outfit wanted weird, offbeat types. So, Neal and his friends went in and acted like lunatics. The crazier they acted, it seemed to Neal, the better Hooper and Henkel liked it.

After the auditions, Henkel spoke to Neal. They wanted him. Neal could hardly believe it. Henkel then told Neal that he thought the movie would be a big success. According to an interview done by John McCarty for his excellent book *Splatter Movies,* Neal had to bite his cheek to keep from laughing. To him, the script seemed ridiculous.

Hooper and Henkel continued their search on campus. They discovered a gentle poet with a dramatic flair, who also happened to be as big as a mountain. Gunnar Hansen was teaching English at the university and editing a poetry magazine. You could not cast more against type than Hansen in the role of Leatherface.

The entire cast came from the University of Texas, or somewhere in the Austin area. It was a talented, underappreciated place in those days. They got Marilyn Burns to play Sally, the only survivor. She was the wife of Bob Burns, who had made the gruesome bone furniture and other props that had been so important in persuading investors to chip in.

While getting his cast together, Hooper was making technical decisions as well. Shooting in 35mm seemed out of the question. Hooper wanted to give himself a lot of leeway for mistakes. He projected his shooting ratio at 10 to 1. Buying that much film stock in 35mm would cost too much. Renting 35mm equipment would be expensive as well. He would have to shoot 16mm, as he did for *Eggshells.*

The camera he selected for the job was one of the best, an Eclair NPR—a self-blimped camera that is used to shoot double-system sound. It is excellent for hand-held shots because of its small size and the magazine placement in back of the camera body instead of on top.

The decision to go the 16mm route would add to the artistic dimensions, as well as the technical and financial. When the film came out, everyone commented on the gritty feel of the images. Some attributed it mistakenly to high-speed 35mm film stock. Of course, Hooper and his cameraman, Daniel Pearl, knew that the blowup from 16mm would give them the look they wanted.

With the budget raised, the cast assembled, and the equipment and props selected, they were ready to start. Hooper had selected locations near Austin. (Why spend money going somewhere else when he had all he needed nearby?) However, the project had jelled at the hottest time of the year. They would be shooting in the Texas summer sun.

Every day the temperature would go over 100 degrees. Those heat-bleached miserable faces you see in the film aren't that way because of craftsmanship. The actors really were hot and miserable.

The heat led to a lot of ill tempers. Marilyn Burns and Paul Partain played brother and sister in the film. (Partain played the wheelchair-bound Franklin.) On the screen, Sally and Franklin bickered constantly. Off screen, they despised each other.

A waking nightmare, Leatherface thunders toward the audience in *The Texas Chainsaw Massacre.*

Rather than hurt the film, their dislike of each other added to its edge. However, there were times when the realism may have gone too far.

One of the most disturbing scenes in the film is when Sally seems to have gotten away from Leatherface. She makes it to the gas station, run by the cook. At this point she doesn't realize that the cook is in cahoots with Leatherface. She thinks she is safe.

The illusion doesn't last for long. Soon, he tries to put her in a sack. When she struggles, he begins to beat her with a broom. When the broom breaks, he starts to thrash her with the handle, a look of glee on his face.

No, Jim Siedow wasn't enjoying what he was doing. The problem was that the phony broom handle didn't look real when he hit her. So, they decided to use the real one. He tried pulling his punches, but that looked no better than before.

To get over the scene, Burns said to go ahead and really hit her with the handle. Siedow started pounding her. The intensity of this scene makes it almost unwatchable. Every one of the blows is real. When the cook thrusts Sally into the truck, she is a beaten wreck. In real life, Marilyn Burns was little better off.

She wasn't the only one getting lumps. Gunnar Hansen, who looked so terrifying in his mask, had difficulty seeing to either side. The mask restricted his vision. As long as he was going straight ahead, he was okay. Going around corners was an adventure. Going around corners wide open, with a roaring chainsaw in his hands, was a kind of percentage game. Sooner or later, he would fall and cut the devil out of himself. All the bumps and bruises he was gathering were the small change of playing the role.

Ed Neal, the hitchhiker, had the privilege of lying on a paved highway in 100-degree temperatures. If you remember the last sequence of the film, you remember that the hitchhiker winds up as roadkill. To get the shots, Neal had to lie on a surface that would literally have fried eggs. In Neal's case, only the side of his face got fried. They tried putting a towel under his head between takes, but it had to come out for the shots.

The painfest reached its apogee on the last day of shooting. Jim Siedow had a previous commitment that he could not break. To get his scenes shot, they had to shoot 26 hours straight. This was the sequence in which the cook, Leatherface, the hitchhiker, and the bound-and-gagged Sally are sitting at the supper table.

There was no air conditioning, no fans, just dead-still Texas air. Meat used as props was turning rotten and stinking. The lights in the small room were right over the actors, roasting them.

One after another, the cast and crew started to get sick. But there was no turning back. The shots had to get done if there was to be a film. People would run to the windows and throw up, then return, head spinning and miserable, ready to do the next take.

Through all the days of shooting, Hooper remained composed. Now, he had his film. But nobody could have predicted what would happen next.

Hooper made a distribution deal with Bryanston Pictures. Bryanston wasn't exactly 20th Century–Fox. Actually, it was one of the sleaziest outfits in the business. The trouble was, none of the majors were interested in horror films. Even smaller distributors shyed away from *Chainsaw;* it was just too intense. Hooper had to do the best he could.

Bryanston did have a track record, of a sort. It had made millions on *Deep Throat.* Another fortune came from *Andy Warhol's Frankenstein.* Bryanston wasn't the sort of company to worry about subject matter. What it cared about was money.

A sneak preview was set up at a San Francisco theater. The main requirement for sneaking a film is that both films have to be of the same rating. You can't sneak an R film for an audience that has come to see a G picture. There are obvious, commonsense reasons for this.

Even if the films have the same rating, the audiences may be wildly different. Here is where the breakdown (or if you are a fan of exploitation campaigns, the setup) came for *Chainsaw.*

The theater was playing the R-rated suspense film *The Taking of Pelham One Two Three.* The audience knew as they entered the theater that a special treat would follow the main feature. They would get to see a sneak preview. Their reaction to the unknown film was considered very important.

There were families in the audience and a pair of city officials. It was a good audience to preview a film for. They watched *The Taking of Pelham One Two Three*, enjoying the mainstream Hollywood offering.

Then the preview began. Oh, those poor people. The titles started over solar flares, then shifted to the hitchhiker's Polaroids from hell. There was no letup. Soon, Leatherface was stocking up the larder with pieces of Kirk, while Pam was impaled on a meathook. Leatherface sat at the window and licked his teeth afterward.

The audience was outraged—at least those who weren't throwing up or hiding under their seats. A gang of them went to find the theater manager to demand their money back. No dice. They had paid their money to see *Pelham*, not the preview. It couldn't be returned.

This was when the fistfight started. A serious little riot was under way when the police and reporters arrived. The two city officials found the reporters and offered to sue on behalf of fellow audience members. The survivors weaved out, stunned at what they had seen.

In other words, *Chainsaw* had gotten the best possible reception. The story of the preview swept the country. Both horror fans and average moviegoers wondered what could have caused such an uproar. A phenomenon was about to start.

When the movie went into general release, critics sought it out, looking for something to lambast in their next day's columns. Many of them had their minds changed. They went in expecting to see a crude gore movie and found something that was a nightmare brought to life. This waking nightmare, this dip into total insanity, was by no means crude. It was a perfectly crafted film that achieved its aims 100 percent.

The public came in droves, attracted by previously mentioned radio ads and print advertising, in addition to the San Francisco preview story. For perhaps the first time in the lives of many viewers, the movie was even stronger than the hype surrounding it. People left the theaters trying to put the movie out of their minds, but found they couldn't. It was the kind of film you had to talk about with your friends, if nothing else just to cleanse your mind. Word of mouth helped pack the theaters.

Everything seemed to be going right for Hooper and *Chainsaw*. It was selected for the Director's Fortnight at Cannes. Some loony thought the film was a fascist attack on youth and called the theater with a bomb threat. There were more headlines and free publicity for *Chainsaw*, this time on an international level. Naturally, the film was banned in France, accused of being an incitement to violence. This just made the other European countries want it that much more.

Still more recognition was on its way. At the Avoriaz Festival, it was awarded the grand prize. But perhaps the most satisfying recognition was the Museum of Modern Art selection of the film for its permanent collection. *Chainsaw* had far outgrown its exploitation roots.

Yet, things only seemed to be going right. *Chainsaw* had, by this time, amassed box office receipts of $20 million. But the investors and actors who had a piece of the film were only getting back peanuts. They turned on Hooper, accusing him of fraud. He was no better off than they were. By now he should have been getting substantial profits. Bryanston was sending him only a fraction of the money it should have been sending.

A lot of standard rip-offs were occurring. For instance, Bryanston would report that a film was playing in two theaters in a city, when it was actually playing four. Whether Bryanston or the local subdistributors were pulling this trick was uncertain.

Considering acts like that, along with *Chainsaw* being booked at scale in many theaters (25 percent of the box office, after advertising costs), the returns to Hooper were reduced to nearly nothing. Then, the big blow came.

Bryanston Pictures dissolved. It simply locked its doors and took off with the money. To this day nobody knows what happened to the millions of dollars *Chainsaw* made in its first release. The only thing that was certain was that Hooper didn't see any of it.

The cast and investors didn't know that. They believed Hooper was responsible. First there were threats, then lawsuits. *Chainsaw* found another distributor, but the deal they got wasn't much better, though the film continued to make money. Soon, the whole mess wound up in the courts. *The Texas Chainsaw Massacre* was withdrawn from circulation. It would be years before it would be shown to the public again. Tobe Hooper's nightmare vision had become a nightmare in real life.

Today, *Chainsaw* is available at every neighborhood video store. It's nice to have it so handy, but on tape it just isn't the same. Something about seeing it in the comfort of your home, where you can look away at the worst times and see familiar things and tell yourself it's just a show on the box takes away from the experience. Also, the lousy quality of the film to video transfer does nothing to help.

People connected with the project have recovered. Gunnar Hansen lampooned the whole mess with his role as the cult leader in *Hollywood Chainsaw Hookers*. Ed Neal returned to the big screen in *Splatter*, costarring Marilyn Burns. Jim Siedow was the only original cast member to act in *Chainsaw, Part Two*.

Hooper has gone on to great fame as one of the top directors in the horror field. He deserves it. Before *Chainsaw*, horror films were shot according to Hitchcock. Suspense was built by warning the audience what might happen, without having the characters know. After *Chainsaw,* the sudden shock was in order.

Actually, Hooper came up with a film in which the tension builds and builds and never lets up. Others might imitate the shocks, but none would ever equal the pace or intensity.

13

Dwain Esper: Exposing a Nation's Shame and Getting Away with It

Of the fans of exploitation who pick up this book, almost all will know the names of Waters, Meyer, and Milligan. They will know some of each man's story. The lives of these men are a part of the lore of the field. But Esper is different.

Yes, people will remember that he made *Maniac* and *Marihuana*, but how much more will they know? For Esper is a part of those shadowy days of exploitation, starting not long after World War I. He was one of the "Forty Thieves." How romantic that sounds. In truth, it was a term used more by police and newspapers than by the men themselves, and often used derisively. Still, it has a ring to it. The Forty Thieves sounds like some sort of organized conspiracy. They weren't. Their connection to each other was no more than that of a group of men, all in the same business, sometimes in competition with each other, all knowing the rest. They knew the larceny in their own hearts well enough to know not to trust each other, yet often managed to con one another just the same.

Esper didn't start out to be that sort of fellow. He was a veteran of World War I. When he got out of the service, he became a successful building contractor. Whatever it was that led him to make the jump from that to filmmaker/roadshow agent has been lost in the decades since.

His next career move was to film production, of a sort. He is thought to have made some of the cheapest silent westerns. Esper's own claim was that he had shot each of them in only two days for just $1,200 a piece. Judging from the quality of some of his later films, this might have been possible. None of these earliest works is known to have survived.

Esper's heyday as a director was the 1930s. The films he made are now regarded as high camp. The dialogue was awful, and the acting worse. Yet, as inept as the films may have been, I think it's wrong to think of Esper as a 1930s Ed Wood.

Esper was out to make a saleable product, a movie that would draw them in at the grindhouses and drive-ins. To do so, he'd have to promise the audience something they couldn't get anywhere else. Of course, even then that was a standard exploitation ploy. But Esper broke the mold. He actually delivered.

He showed drug use, sex scenes that looked like the opening of a stag film, and even the greatest taboo of the day: nudity. When almost nobody else had the guts to do it, Dwain Esper was slipping nude scenes into his films.

Maniac is one of his best-known movies from that period. In it, a mad scientist decides to perform a heart transplant. He and his assistant steal a woman's body from the morgue to use as part of their experiment. First, they have to revive her. It wasn't enough to just transplant a heart, they were going to raise the dead, too.

This scene didn't exactly come off like Dr. Frankenstein giving life to his creation, electricity shooting everywhere. Esper just didn't have the money for fancy lab equipment. His mad Dr. Meierschultz resurrects the dead woman with a simple massage. It is impossible to describe just how lame this looks.

Now they need another body. Dr. Meierschultz sends out his assistant, Maxwell, to fetch another one. When Maxwell fails, Meierschultz decides to kill him. But Maxwell does in the mad doctor instead. He takes over the doctor's identity and starts performing loony experiments of his own.

Not quite having as good a handle on these things as the doctor did, Maxwell goofs, injecting one fellow with a drug that makes him think he's the ape in Poe's *Murders in the Rue Morgue*. The man grabs the woman they revived earlier and runs off into the woods with her. Esper uses the chance to slip in a nude shot, showing the woman's breasts.

Through the filming of his epic, Esper had the help of another Hollywood legend, William C. Thompson. Thompson would later be cinematographer on *Plan 9 from Outer Space*. It's sort of amazing that one person could be connected to two such bombs. Thompson wasn't a bad cinematographer. Given the chance, as in *Daughter of Horror*, he could do a genuinely good job. With *Maniac*, he did as good a job as most other low-budget films of the period.

When Esper saw the final print of *Maniac*, he knew he didn't have a masterpiece, but he believed the public would go for his wild tale. With the help of Louis Sonney, another member of the Forty Thieves, now a legend himself, Esper put the film into the theaters.

It died. The film just wasn't doing any business. Esper and Sonney were in danger of losing their investment. Though no great fortune had been spent, Esper's filmmaking career was a shoestring existence, a shoestring that was getting very frayed.

Maniac was a bust, until Esper retitled it *Sex Maniac*.

Perhaps one reason for the film's poor showing was its trailer. This wonderful piece of film that bad movie buffs treasure today was no big deal then. Mostly what the audience saw was something about a mad scientist and a lot of hammy acting. There were a lot of movies about mad scientists. And they had good actors in them.

But there weren't many movies about sex fiends or injections with strange drugs, and there were very, very few with breasts. Esper and Sonney redid the trailer and their promotional campaign. They retitled the film *Sex Maniac* and started raking in the money.

The profits helped fund the most prolific three years in Esper's career. Esper would make short subjects like *How to Undress in Front of Your Husband*, *March of Crime*, and *Narcotic*. *Narcotic* touched on a favorite film subject of his, illegal drug use. He would use the subject best in his feature, *Marihuana: Weed with Roots in Hell*.

Esper had learned his lesson well on *Maniac*. With *Marihuana*, he would serve up depravity of all sorts and be shockingly graphic about it, at least for the 1930s.

In the sleaziest exploitation films of the period, there would be a scene of women starting to undress. The audience would lean forward in their seats, wanting to catch every little bit, because they knew the film would cut away before the women actually got naked.

Esper pulled a trick on the audience. He held the shot, as more and

Esper promised plenty, like all the exploitation crowd. But unlike them, he delivered.

more clothes came off. Finally, at the last instant, when every other film would cut away, leaving the audience at least reasonably satisfied, Esper didn't. He went all the way. The last undergarments popped off, and guys in the audience fell out of their seats. Those women were really naked.

Esper didn't stop there. He had all the women run outside and jump in the water for a midnight skinny-dipping scene. In the two or three other films that were around that were brave enough to try something like this, the most anybody saw was a flash of some woman's bare heinie as she swam along the surface. Not Esper. He had them running around and splashing about, with the camera taking it all in.

This sequence led to one of my favorite lines in the film. The one where the fellow has found out about the wild party that took place. His voice fills with conviction, as he stares straight into the camera.

"Police will pass an innocent weenie roast on the beach, but if they learn there's been a drinking party and nude bathing, an investigation will surely take place!"

Esper filmed this little speech head-on, in close-up. It just screams to the audience, "I didn't have any money to do this right, so I did it any way I could." It has the look of a shot Esper did when nobody else was available, so he just stuck the guy in front of the camera and had him say his lines.

Esper knew the speeches didn't matter. It was the chance to see a little skin that would pull in the crowds. The skin, though, would prove to be a problem.

No matter how well the picture educated the public on the evils of marijuana (it didn't; with all the girls, and wild times, guys probably came out of the theater wondering where they could get hold of the stuff), some theaters refused to play it. The nudity went too far.

A censored version was prepared, as well as a more conservative trailer. Some places were willing, even eager, to play the movie version with nudity, but not the trailer that showed the girls shucking their clothes off. They worried that patrons who came to see a family picture might be offended when this coming attraction flashed on the screen.

Esper still managed to slip in a glimpse of nudity. In the shot where the girls run out of the house, you can't see any nudity directly. But if you look in the mirror in the upper right-hand corner, there they are. Esper knew how to get his message out. If you came to see this picture, you'd see something.

Another type of movie that pulled audiences into the theaters in those long-ago days were what have come to be known as "birth of a baby" pictures. The climax of the film would be medical footage of childbirth. The most famous of these films is Kroger Babb's *Mom and Dad*, but Dwain Esper had one out at least 15 years before Babb's.

Called *Modern Motherhood,* like all the rest of the "birth of a baby" pictures, it warned that ignorance led to teenage pregnancy. Again, under the guise of educating the public, Esper was filling his pockets.

Unfortunately for fans of camp, Esper's filmmaking activities tailed off after his three-year burst in the 1930s. While his movies had never exactly been polished productions, audiences didn't reject them. They came to see forbidden fruit. The more experienced among them came to see if the movies would actually deliver what the ads and trailers said. Esper's did. He didn't have any trouble getting them into the theaters.

Top: A still from *Freaks*. Esper would retitle it *Forbidden Love* and *Nature's Mistakes*. *Bottom:* Some of the gentle cast of *Freaks*.

Dwain Esper's "platform" still allowed him to show plenty of hot stuff and to rake in the cash. Promo for *Modern Motherhood*.

Getting paid was another matter. There was no end to the number of rip-offs in the business. Even when everything was on the up and up, the exhibitor and the distributor came away with most of the profits. Esper's own experience, roadshowing his own films, told him where the real money was. Most of the rest of his career would be spent in this line.

Nothing exists today that compares to the old practice of roadshowing films. It was a technique in which one man could shoot a film and be its agent, deliveryman, and even its projectionist, while tallying up the box office take. Though some, like Kroger Babb, made big business of roadshowing, the best understanding of it can come from looking at the career of a one-man band like Esper.

The first step to roadshowing a film was to establish a route, that is, to book the film into a number of theaters and drive-ins. To do so, the roadshow man put on his agent's hat and went to the offices of the theater chains. Ideally, he would get the film booked in one theater to play a certain date and when that date was up, his next booking would be perhaps a day's drive away. He would try to get a series of bookings to fill perhaps 20 weeks.

Independent theater and drive-in owners were just as important to the roadshow agent as were the big chains. Often they were more receptive to their risqué offerings than the chains were. The agent would be sure to drive through the hinterlands, scouting them out, striking as many deals for playdates as he could. Some agents made their entire routes of independent theaters. Drive-ins were particularly sought after.

With his season's route set, the roadshow man would set out. If he worked for a big outfit, mass mailings of circulars to post office boxes and rural routes would herald the coming of his film. If he was by himself, he might slip into town as unnoticed as a fly. Most managed to prepurchase some advertising in the local newspaper.

These ads were of great importance. In that day, newspapers allowed ads that were a bit more lurid than they do today. As long as nothing obscene was shown or said in the ads, they could get away with about anything. Of course, they made the most sensational claims and warned patrons that the films were only for adult audiences. That is, unless it was a "birth of a baby" picture. Then parents would be admonished to see it with their teenagers.

As the crowd started to show up for the movie, the roadshow man tried to keep an eye on the box office. He would usually have booked his film at a percentage rate, and it would pay to see that no little tricks were going on.

Then the movie would start. That the film often was an old chestnut wasn't enough to get the audience ticked off. At that time, particularly drive-in crowds were accustomed to seeing films years after their initial release. If, as the night wore on, none of the promised depravity was shown on the screen, then the crowd might get a little testy.

Esper and other experienced roadshow men kept a little something handy for such occasions. It was called a square-up reel, usually nudist camp footage or a burlesque short. It was called a square-up reel because it literally squared things up with the audience. The roadshow man would first check for police, then if the coast was clear, he'd have the projectionist put on the reel.

Square-up reels were a necessity of the trade, but they were risky. The crowd left feeling like it got its money's worth, and considering the rarity of such footage then, they had. Of course, they would go and tell their friends what they'd seen. A bigger crowd would be back the next day. The roadshow man and the theater owner loved that. The trouble was that the cops might be in the crowd.

The cops might confiscate the print of his movie, throw him in the pokey, or just create a big stink for the theater owner. Any of the above was bad news and might have other theaters on his route drop him. So the square-up reel had to be used judiciously.

Esper spent the next several years bumping about the country, living this sort of life, showing his own films and those of other filmmakers. His path would cross others of the Forty Thieves, sometimes pleasantly, other times not.

One of the strangest was the episode of the FBI poster. Theater owners and film bookers all over the country started receiving FBI Wanted posters with Esper's name and picture on them. Often, they would reach a booker's office just about the time Esper was due in to try to book his film. When the startled bookers called the FBI, they discovered that Esper wasn't wanted for anything.

Esper went for weeks with the phony FBI posters dogging him everywhere. People tried to turn him in. The bookers viewed him suspiciously. Considering he was the kind of fellow who went wandering around the country, showing sleaze movies, it was easy to believe bad things about him.

It was not until several years later that the truth was learned. It turned out that the posters were being mailed by "Pappy" Golden, another of the Forty Thieves. He was doing it either to hurt Esper's business or from sheer devilment. By most accounts, Golden was the sort of fellow who would have thought the posters were a fine joke.

In 1949, Esper would get the rights to a long-suppressed classic, *Freaks*. Tod Browning's film had so shocked audiences upon its release in 1932 that MGM pulled it from circulation. Few theaters would play this tale set in the world of a circus freak show, which used real freaks as its cast.

Esper guessed correctly that a more adventurous movie-going public existed in 1949. He bought the film for peanuts, then gave it the racy title *Forbidden Love*. His ads made all manner of wild promises about what the film contained. He took the movie out on the road and started raking in the profits.

But Esper saw even more profit potential in *Freaks*. He retitled it *Nature's Mistakes* and then recruited a real freak show to travel the country with it. The members of the freak show would set up shop in the theater lobbies, and the audience would file past as they went in to see the movie. Esper kept them on the road for five years.

Although it sounds outrageous, it was nothing more than traveling shows had been doing for hundreds of years. But in his next venture, Esper crossed the line, exploiting the most base, morbid curiosity of man. He released his infamous *Atrocities of War*.

Esper had collected some of the most brutal footage to come out of World War II. These graphic scenes of the Nazi death camps were edited into a feature-length documentary. There had been other entries in the "shockumentary" field, but none that staggered audiences the way this one did.

After his experiences with the traveling freak show and *Nature's Mistakes,* he was convinced of the drawing power of a lobby show or similar added attractions. He searched out a 1937 Mercedes, claimed it was Hitler's car, and put it on the road with the film.

14

Andy Milligan: Period Dramas for Under $10,000

If you tell people the kind of budgets Andy Milligan makes films on, they will scoff. Even your friends who aren't movie buffs will know better. It's just not possible to make a film for this kind of money. Movies cost millions of dollars to make. Now, a low-budget one may be a few hundred thousand dollars, but $10,000? It sounds like he filmed a high school play.

Now consider this: Most of his films are period pieces, with realistic costumes, settings, and props. It would seem that he spends his entire budget merely on renting costumes. Yet, he pays for film stock, lab fees, his cast, and everything else out of this microscopic (by filmmaking terms) sum.

How has he managed it? If you want to learn the art of ultra-low-budget filmmaking, particularly the kind practiced in the 1960s and 1970s, there is no better guide than the career of Andy Milligan.

Milligan was a young businessman in the garment industry who yearned to make films. The world of the garment trade produces a certain kind of go-getter, a fellow who is willing to take a risk when the chance for profit is there. Milligan knew of the big money being raked in by low-budget films. He wanted in on it, but not for the money alone.

He was a man with a creative mind in a business that just didn't have much room for creativity, at least not at the level he was involved at. Judging by what was out there, about anybody could be a filmmaker. Of course, you needed equipment.

On the creative side of filmmaking, Milligan knew a great deal. He knew the kinds of stories he could tell and how he wanted them to look. Making them was another matter. Here, he was a greenhorn. You obviously needed a camera, but what kind?

He had a friend named Art Ford. Ford was a disc jockey with a longtime interest in all aspects of filmmaking, including the technical side. Ford knew that Milligan would be virtually a one-man-band kind of filmmaker. He would need a camera that would record sound on the film itself, rather than one that required a separate recorder. Also, he would benefit if the camera had a large magazine, so once it was loaded, he wouldn't have to fumble about reloading it.

Ford recommended the Auricon, a popular news camera of the day. It was so expensive that it just about required you to have the backing of a television station to buy one. A new one cost several thousand dollars, even in the early 1960s; however, there were bargains to be found if you were willing to buy a used camera. Since New York is a camera hunter's Mecca, he was able to scout out a high-quality Auricon for only $800.

There was a drawback. The camera lacked magnetic recording heads. It was equipped to do sound, but only old-fashioned optical sound. Optical sound, in unskilled hands, has laid low a lot of film projects. Milligan resolved to do the best he could.

With little more than a camera, microphone, and some lights, Milligan was ready to try making a feature. If he went through the typical course of making short experimental films beforehand, there is no proof of it today. It seems that Milligan had his mind set on making a feature and would not be turned away.

It would be a tough road, which a surprising number of potential filmmakers have tried and most of them have failed. Milligan would not.

He shot film for four months whenever he could grab the time. Weekends filled most of his shooting schedule, such as it was. Working with an amateur cast, all of whom had lives and needs of their own, meant juggling scenes and locations so that people could be there. It was a hectic time, filled with the joys of filmmaking, such as seeing rushes of shots that turned out just right, and the aggravations of dealing with a hundred tiny details. He had to deal with the problems himself because he never had a crew of more than four or five people, and they were often trying to learn as they went.

Milligan pressed on and was finally able to complete his film. He titled it *Liz*. All the while, he had run his regular business, kept his "normal" life going. There wasn't much choice. He had made the film with $7,500 of his own money.

Here is another lesson for the young filmmaker. You don't have to have a million dollars to make a film. You do have to be smart; talented; and, above all, willing to work as long as it takes, as hard as it takes. The last quality will serve you best, as it did Milligan.

The next step lay before him. He had to find a distributor. Most filmmakers do a film with some sort of distribution deal prearranged. However, in the depths of the exploitation field, it's more the rule that a first timer like Milligan would do his work on speculation.

This may seem a tremendous risk, even with the tiny budget Milligan had to gamble. But he had done his homework. Movies were starting to break new ground. Strange delights were being offered to the exploitation fans, as well as to the general movie-going public. People were running around naked in films. And saying things never before used in films. One of the last taboos, that of the four-letter word, was being broken.

Milligan sprinkled his film with these elements, using just enough to get *Liz* noticed, he hoped.

Filmmakers usually shop their film around to one distributor at a time. It can be a time-consuming process. Milligan decided to speed things up by holding a screening of his film and inviting every distributor he thought might be interested. He didn't depend on any inside contacts or special information to find the distributors he wanted to invite. He just picked up the phone book and started to dial.

With this kind of cold-calling approach from a total unknown, you might think a lot of people hung up on him. Perhaps they did. But enough people showed an interest in his project to make it seem that the screening was a good idea.

The big day came. Only four distributors showed up. Milligan had spent hours going through the phone book, making at least 30 calls. And these were the smallest distributors, names nobody had ever heard of. Well, he had told them he was going to have a screening, so he would show them the film.

The projector was started, and *Liz* unspooled before them. What started off as a disappointment began to turn into a success. The little group liked the film. One distributor liked it more than the rest. His name was William Mishkin.

Though not widely known, Bill Mishkin was a name in the little pond of exploitation films. He had distributed everything from science fiction to sex films, consistently making money on movies for the drive-in and grindhouse circuit.

Mishkin wanted the film, but to play the kind of markets he had, the film needed more nudity. Milligan wasn't sure about this advice. He decided to ignore Mishkin and try again.

It might seem strange for a person with a $7,500 movie to turn away from what amounted to an offer to distribute his film, if he would add a few shots. But you must keep in mind that Milligan had struggled for months with his little movie, that he had beaten the odds to get it this far. What he wanted to hear was that somebody liked his film as it was.

At his next screening, a few other distributors showed up. Among them was the persistent Mishkin.

This time, it didn't go so well. The group seemed indifferent to his effort. Milligan was beginning to realize what he had on his hands. A $7,500 feature, an animal that by rights shouldn't even exist. An animal that only one person wanted.

Mishkin was still as enthusiastic as ever. Milligan gave in, telling Mishkin he would add the scenes he wanted. There would be four such scenes, each just a few seconds long. That was all it took for Mishkin to be satisfied. He was ready to get Milligan's film into the theaters.

One other change had to be made. *Liz* was just not an exploitation title. They needed something that would draw the public in at the grindhouses. They decided to call it *The Promiscuous Sex*.

At New York's infamous World Theater, it ran for 29 weeks, lining up the customers every day. Mishkin put it on the road with similar success.

It would seem that Milligan struck gold on his first try. He didn't. An explanation of distribution deals will show why.

When a theater books a film, it usually books it at a percentage of the gross. For independents like Milligan, this usually turns out to be 25 percent. The distributor gets half this 25 percent, leaving the producer with only 12.5 percent of the gross. In such a deal, the distributor and the producer split the costs of prints and their share of the advertising bill. By now, the producer is getting less than 10 percent of the gross.

Another way to look at it is this: Milligan was getting less than one dollar in ten that the theaters took in. And the theaters were taking their time paying, which unfortunately was the usual custom.

Milligan wasn't getting ripped off, no more than anyone else. But for an independent filmmaker to strike it rich, his film must be a phenomenal success.

Since Milligan didn't want to pick up where he had left off in the garment business, he needed another film project. Mishkin could always use another movie to distribute, particularly if he could get it cheap. You might think that with the success of *The Promiscuous Sex*, Mishkin might have advanced Milligan a somewhat bigger budget in hopes of getting a better film. If you think that, you don't know Mishkin.

A $7,500 picture had been good enough to draw in the crowds the first time. His reasoning must have been, why spend any more than that?

So he offered Milligan exactly what he had spent to piece together the first one, $7,500. There were no strings attached; Milligan could make anything he wanted to as long as it was exploitation.

Milligan grabbed the money. Though it was a pittance, he had worked that way on his first film. He went off to New Jersey and made his first horror film, *The Naked Witch*. Shooting full time, he was able to complete the movie in just eight days.

The plot was perhaps influenced by those of Hammer Films and Roger Corman's Poe cycle. A witch, executed in the 1800s, spreads her evil to modern times, gaining control of a young college student. Milligan believed he was headed for success.

Still, Milligan had no set deal with anyone, other than his agreement with Mishkin for *The Naked Witch*. While he was editing his footage in a rented booth, three men came along and saw him at work. They ran a company called ASA.

ASA made films a bit more expensive than the kind Milligan made; $60,000 a movie was their speed. They had just finished such a film for distributor Jerry Balsam.

That they were more expensive doesn't mean they were any better. As a matter of fact, Milligan, with his backyard production techniques, was turning out a better product. The ASA fellows quickly noticed that.

They didn't tell Milligan how much their last film cost to make or that they were connected to Jerry Balsam. But they did want to know how much Milligan had spent on his. When he told them $7,500 each, the ASA gang hatched a plot.

You see, ASA owed Jerry Balsam a huge sum of money, which they had zero chance of repaying. Now if they had some films that would turn a profit just by getting booked into a few theaters, then they might be able to stay in business. Without any knowledge of what he was getting into, Milligan signed on to do three pictures for ASA.

Milligan faithfully turned out the three films on peanut budgets and sat back, hoping for the money to start coming his way. After all, three movies, even if they played only inner-city theaters and a few Southern drive-ins, should provide a decent living.

Not a cent came in. It turned out that Balsam had gotten tired of waiting for ASA to pay up. He confiscated ASA's assets, of which about the only worthwhile ones were Milligan's films. Milligan was left out in the cold. Eventually, he received a settlement of $1,000 per film, a total of only $3,000 for movies that would make a profit in the neighborhood of a quarter of a million dollars.

Among the movies, *The Depraved, The Degenerates,* and *The Ghastly Ones,* one is particularly noteworthy. *The Ghastly Ones* was Milligan's first movie that was entirely a period piece. It demonstrates Milligan's skill at wringing every penny's worth of value out of a dollar.

Milligan found a quiet old home nearby on Staten Island that would serve as his setting, a country estate in the late 1800s. Every person would have to be appropriately costumed. His background in the garment business served him well; he made many of the costumes himself. After he was through with the costumes for one film, he saved them for the next.

Equipment rental was no problem. He owned his own gear, the faithful Auricon. Owning the means of production cut as much as $2,000 from the budget of the film. Camera and light packages are expensive to rent.

Though the special effects were convincingly gory, they were strictly of the clay and animal innards school, pioneered by H. G. Lewis. His entire effects budget probably didn't exceed $100.

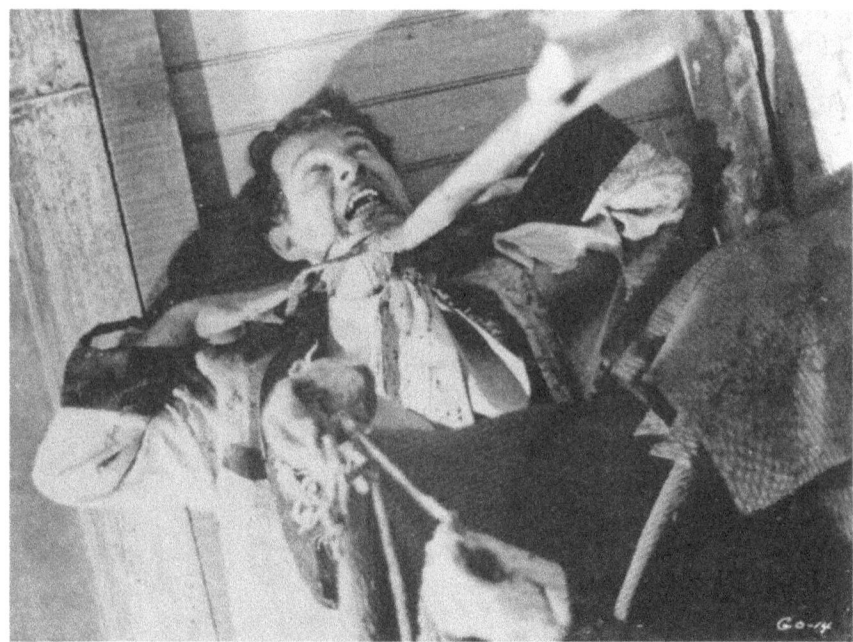

This still from *The Ghastly Ones* shows off Milligan's simple, but effective gore effects.

In only a short time in the business, Milligan had learned how to cut every corner and still turn out films that were winners. Poverty had been a great teacher. Now he needed someone who would give him a chance to make a better picture—someone who would give him long-term stability, so he wouldn't have to worry about where financing for his next movie was coming from.

Jerry Balsam did what seemed like one good thing for Milligan. He introduced him to the owner of Cinemania Films, Leslie Elliot. Elliot knew all about Milligan. As a distributor in Great Britain, Cinemania had handled most of Milligan's films, getting them through William Mishkin. Elliot offered him a deal calling for three pictures a year for the next five years.

It was just what Milligan was looking for. As part of the arrangement, he would move to London, home of the masters of period horror, Hammer Films. Of course, he wouldn't have anywhere near the resources that company had, but he would have authentic settings right at hand.

As soon as he got to London, he started to work. Never a fellow to mess around, he shot two movies, *Nightbirds* and *The Body Beneath*. Then, disaster struck.

Leslie Elliot wasn't the sole owner of Cinemania. His father was the real power in the company, and he didn't like Milligan's films or the deal

Milligan's use of period costumes and sets was remarkable, considering his tiny budgets. From *Bloodthirsty Butchers*.

his son had made with Milligan. Milligan found himself with a contract that was worthless. Fortunately, the two films he made were still his.

While he waited for the situation with Cinemania to clarify, he took advantage of his English settings to make two films for Mishkin, *Bloodthirsty Butchers* and *Curse of the Full Moon*.

Once the miserable business with Cinemania was taken care of, Milligan was ready to come home. Despite the five-year deal coming apart, he came out of it better than when he went in. He was bringing four movies back to the United States with him. One was to become a masterpiece of strangeness at the hands of Mishkin.

In Milligan's absence, a horror movie had swept the country. *Willard*, the story of a young man and the army of rats he trains to do his bidding, was breaking the box office. Mishkin had to get in on the action.

Curse of the Full Moon was a werewolf picture that had about as little to do with rats as a movie could. No matter to Mishkin. He had Milligan shoot some rat scenes on Staten Island and tagged them onto the end of the film. He entitled the resulting atrocity *The Rats Are Coming, the Werewolves Are Here*.

Unlike many of his contemporaries in the exploitation field, Milligan's filmmaking career continues to this day. Though the late 1970s and early 1980s were a time of reduced production for him, the lure of video dollars has brought him back. One of his latest films, *Weirdo* may be his best.

This story, of a slightly retarded boy who falls in love with a crippled girl, is just as schmaltzy as it sounds. Yet, Milligan makes it all work by being surprisingly frank in his treatment. In case you think Milligan has turned away from his exploitation roots, guess again. *Weirdo* is a schmaltz-gore film! When the young man, who has been tormented through the film by just about everybody, has finally had enough, the payoff comes. While the killings are either accidental or in self-defense, the blood flows and heads are sent rolling. Those who watch this gem will be proud to note that Milligan's f/x are still as delightfully crude as they were in 1970.

15

Larry Buchanan: Does Mars Need Women That Badly?

There are directors of legend in the exploitation field. Men who could whip out finished films one after another in only a few days time. It is one thing for an exploitation pro to shoot a film in a week when he has had months to prepare. It is entirely another to fire one off and then start shooting another the very next day, with a script that has just been handed to him.

Of this select group, people like William Beaudine and Lee "Roll 'em" Sholem come to mind. Also, in this hearty group must be numbered Larry Buchanan.

From 1966 to 1968, Buchanan churned out a cycle of unforgettable monster films, with titles like *Zontar: The Thing from Venus* and *Mars Needs Women*. Their importance isn't that they were great films or even good films. Like the men just mentioned, Buchanan had to turn out a film, any kind of film, in a set time, on a budget that would make the director of a 15-second commercial weep. The remarkable thing was that he did it every time. He never missed a deadline or went over budget.

Of course, Buchanan didn't set out in life to become a movie-making machine. Actually, he didn't have a promising start at all.

Buchanan was born the son of a Texas Ranger. He would never truly know his family. He was orphaned at the age of four and placed in a Baptist institution.

Being an imaginative child, he did not enjoy the strict upbringing the institution dished out. As did so many others in similar circumstances, he sought relief through the movies. But Buchanan was not a retreating child, who lived merely through his dreams. He boldly said he wanted to be a filmmaker. When the chance at a minister's scholarship to Baylor University was offered, he turned it down to try his hand at films.

The subject of his first attempt was a logical one for a young man brought up by the Baptists. A tent revival was starting in 1951. It would be led by a then little-known preacher named Oral Roberts. Buchanan would film it.

Buchanan knew all the ins and outs of the pray-for-pay crowd. Even then, in its crude "pass the collection plate and hope for a good haul" days, Buchanan saw the manipulation of poor, honest people and was sickened by it. He decided to give up on documentaries for the time being, (although it was a format he would put to use effectively in later years) and go to Hollywood.

Here, luck and a bit of hard work would pay off. Some people spend years in Hollywood struggling for a break and never getting one. In only a few months, Buchanan would become assistant to George Cukor on the film *The Marrying Kind*. In addition, he started to capture small roles as an actor.

For a young man just in from Texas, he was doing very well, indeed. The chance to work with Cukor gave him valuable insight as to how Hollywood filmmaking really worked. And while the roles he got weren't large, the movies were top line A features—films like *The Ox-Bow Incident, The Gunfighter,* and *Coming in on the Wings of a Prayer.*

Still, this wasn't what he had aimed for. Though he was a part of making films, he wasn't making them himself. He wasn't the man in charge. What he saw in Hollywood didn't give him a lot of faith in the notion that he'd be in that position any time soon.

In addition, while he had been comparatively successful, things he had seen along the way had not endeared him to the Hollywood system. Parts of it were as bad as the tent-revival world he had escaped. If he was going to make films, he'd have to do it on his own.

Those who like biographies to follow a logical course may start putting facts together from Buchanan's past to chart his next step. He came from a religious background, he worked in Hollywood; that probably means he would have decided on a religious film as his first project. Far from it. The title: *The Naked Witch*.

Like many another of decent background, when he made the jump to independent production, he decided on the surprising route of sexploitation films. It made sense. For the lowest possible investment, he could get a film in the can that would almost certainly make money. For the first-time filmmaker, this was all important.

Buchanan would go on to make a string of films for this market that hold the admiration of exploitation fans to this day. It was his gutsy choice of material, which utterly screamed out bad taste in its search for the box office dollar, that makes these movies favorites.

One example is *Naughty Dallas*. Now, unless you are a historian, that title probably rings no bell. But not that many years ago, those words held

Poster for *Naughty Dallas*. Those interested in the assassination of John F. Kennedy will note the names of Jack Ruby's clubs: The Colony Club and the Carousel. As the poster says, Jada is featured in the film. She is the woman who said Jack Ruby introduced her to Lee Harvey Oswald a month before the assassination. Like many others with information related to the case, she would die within a short time.

a strange fascination for the public—a public that was obsessed with one of its greatest tragedies.

President John F. Kennedy was assassinated by Lee Harvey Oswald, who, in turn, was assassinated by Jack Ruby. No one who was watching television that day will ever forget that scene. When the reporters finally sorted things out, they tried to tell us who Jack Ruby was. On most television stations, the description didn't go beyond "night club owner." But through other sources, the word began to get out to the country. Jack Ruby owned strip-tease joints.

Buchanan took footage he had shot in Ruby's clubs and put it on the road in 1964. I honestly do not believe that he meant any disrespect in his choice of subject matter. There was a lot of curiosity about the places. And one did happen to be in his hometown.

Among Buchanan's other movies from this period was a landmark blaxploitation film, *Free, White, and 21*. Some people refer to it as the first blaxploitation movie, though this is a hard shot to call. Exploitation films targeted at blacks had been around since the 1930s. To say it was the first of the modern wave that began in the 1960s may be more accurate.

His next effort in blaxploitation is almost as well known and stayed on the road probably longer. *High Yellow*, shot in 1965, was still playing inner-city theaters almost ten years later.

The titles themselves are classics of exploitation. A low-budget filmmaker like Buchanan had to work every angle that he could. There was no allowance for a weak, bland title. Hollywood might be able to spend huge sums to promote a movie with an ordinary title, fill it with stars, and open it in movie palaces. In these circumstances, a fellow like Buchanan had to grab people with his titles and say "Here it is, guys. This is a movie that's going to stir up some trouble."

Making movies on tiny budgets and supplying them with regularity to distributors like AIP, was winning Buchanan a good reputation in the business. Dependability is a rare commodity in the filmmaking trade and an essential one for the success of shoestring productions. Soon, AIP would have an opportunity that Buchanan was ideal for.

The ABC television network was looking for filler material that could be used late at night, Saturday afternoons, and other times when viewership was low. Ordinarily, it would use reruns of shows canceled years before or old movies of a sort there will probably never be a cult for.

The network decided to be innovative. If someone could supply it with new material, of a sort that did have some built-in interest, at a low price, ABC would use it. It didn't matter if it was really good or not. It just had to be competently made. This material could be played against the competition when they were running worn-out things and at least have the advantage of newness.

AIP was known as America's biggest producer of B movie fare. Would they be interested in making movies for television? Not B movies or even C movies, but somewhere lower still. Say, about a D.

AIP would. But for the kind of money ABC was offering, the movies couldn't be shot in Hollywood. AIP would have to go to an out-of-town producer, the kind who could shoot a movie with a five- or six-man crew and, if necessary, do any of the jobs himself. A fellow like Larry Buchanan.

AIP originally signed Buchanan to a three-picture contract. (It should be noted that it was getting movies from other producers for the ABC deal as well.) It would be the start of his monster cycle, and the start of much of the filmmaking business in Dallas that is thriving today.

It was a humble beginning. Since the average budget for these films was only $22,000, there wasn't any money for a new script. However, AIP owned the rights to a lot of scripts that had already been shot. In effect, it was asking Buchanan to do zero-budget remakes of low-budget films.

The first project AIP sent his way was *The Eye Creatures*—the same script AIP had shot in 1957 as *Invasion of the Saucer Men*. There was a UFO flap going on at the time, so the subject must have seemed like a natural.

Usually, if a director is doing a remake of a successful film, he keeps the same subject matter and the same basic story line, but feels free to tell the story the way he wants to. On *The Eye Creatures* there would be no time for any of this foolishness. If AIP wanted a remake of *Invasion of the Saucer Men*, then it would get one. In Buchanan's version, the only changes were different actors and cheaper sets. Otherwise, it was an across-the-board, scene-by-scene reshooting of the original. There was no time or money to figure out a different way.

Many point fingers of derision at Buchanan's monster films, giving them "Golden Turkey Awards," laughing at their chintziness. It was the lack of money and of resources of all kinds that laid these films low. The tales of what Buchanan had to do to make up for these shortcomings is where the real humor lies. Take *The Eye Creatures*.

Buchanan was able to get two good monster suits. These were the kind that would scare the pants off all the seven year olds in the audience and even grab the attention of their parents. The problem was, the script called for eight invaders. Somehow, he had to come up with six more monster suits.

The problem wasn't so bad as it seemed, not if you were Larry Buchanan and had never had more than about a $1.50 to shoot a film with anyway. What he would do was use the two good suits on his lead monsters and whenever he had to do a closeup. Still, there would be group shots. This was supposed to be an invasion, and two monsters weren't much of an invasion.

His answer would have been ingenious if it had worked. He got six wetsuits and decorated them a little. He figured that since the group scenes came at night, nobody would be able to tell the difference. All the audience would be able to see was an outline.

To get the scenes shot as quickly and cheaply as possible, Buchanan decided to shoot day for night. It was this last little bit of cheapness that clobbered him.

In day-for-night shooting the filmmaker does exactly that. He shoots a nighttime scene during the day. To make it look like night, he either closes down the f-stop of the lens, so less light gets to the film, or uses a dark filter. Carefully shot, such a scene gives a passable rendition of night when projected on a theater screen.

The trouble was, the movie was going to be shown on television. Here, a device called an automatic scanner comes into play. Simply put, the scanner reads the film image, so the signal can be converted to video. It also automatically sets the light levels for each scene. When it saw Buchanan's day-for-night shots, it burped. That is, it misread them as daylight scenes. The light levels went up, and six wetsuits were revealed in all their shoddy glory.

People laugh at these shots to this day. Some people I know have watched *The Eye Creatures* for no other reason. But it isn't as easy as it seems.

Shooting night for night is expensive. It requires lights, generators, cables, and people to take care of the mess. And there wasn't exactly a surplus of equipment or qualified operators in Dallas at that time.

For Buchanan, starting a film was about the same as opening a film school. Not only did he have to produce and direct his projects, he had to teach everybody their jobs. This has been a time-honored tradition in exploitation films. A lot of people got their first jobs in the industry working for Buchanan.

S. F. "Brownie" Brownrigg started with him as a soundman. Within a few years, he would be a producer in his own right, doing such exploitation classics as *Don't Look in the Basement, Keep My Grave Open,* and *Poor White Trash 2*. Similarly, Robert Jessop was getting the chance to watch the flickering images in the viewfinder of Buchanan's camera. Jessop would go on to be the most sought-after cameraman in Dallas.

But these triumphs were years in the future. Buchanan himself would know acclaim. For now, he had monsters with Ping-Pong balls for eyes and not enough lights to shoot them with.

Buchanan might have trouble with lighting, but he wasn't short of crafty ways of getting around it. Take the movie *Mars Needs Women,* for example.

You'll notice that several of the scenes look murky. Buchanan had nowhere near the time or equipment needed to shoot them right. Nowadays, filmmakers can make up for poor lighting by using faster film stock.

One common type is 16mm film made to shoot at ASA 500 or higher. The film in use then was typically rated ASA 25.

To make it look good, you needed a lot of lights. But Buchanan didn't have to make it look good. He just had to get acceptable results.

So he beat the problem by undercranking the camera. Instead of shooting at 24 frames per second (fps), he shot at 18 and, in some cases, as low as 12. This let more light into the film, giving him an image.

Now any of you who have seen the old silent movies that were shot and meant to be projected at 12 fps or so can see the problem this was leading to. When those old silents are projected at 24 fps, the actors double time it across the screen, their motions all jerky. Never doubt Buchanan though.

To compensate, he told his actors to move v-e-r-y s-l-o-w-l-y. However, since each person might interpret this order differently, the motions still aren't quite right. But somehow, in this movie such things seem to fit.

Mars Needs Women was shot on what for Buchanan was a leisurely two-week shooting schedule. The record for his monster cycle films was six days for *It's Alive*. The turn-around time between films was often minimal.

AIP would call Buchanan and tell him what was wanted. The script might arrive the next day by special delivery. He would read through it, blocking the shots and tossing out anything he couldn't fit into his tiny budget. The next day, he would start shooting.

Of course, it didn't always go like this. The films weren't all shot back to back. Still, Buchanan did keep up a furious pace, averaging seven films a year.

Having continually to do remakes of other people's films was getting to him. He was able to slip in his own stuff now and then, films like *Strawberries Need Rain,* but not enough. He had had enough Eye Creatures and Zontars to do him for a while. He finished up his batch of television films with a war movie, *Hell Raiders*.

Now he would call on his past experience as a documentary filmmaker to gain recognition and respect. He would make dramas with the raw edge of documentary films in the new genre called docudrama.

Notable among these are films like *The Trial of Lee Harvey Oswald*. Made long before television started its wave of movies related to the assassination, Buchanan showed that he was keeping his ears open to what the public wanted. Speakers were visiting college campuses, drawing standing-room crowds, talking about the assassination and Oswald. Books and newspaper articles were being written. Buchanan took the "what if" angle to examine the crime, Oswald, and how the country might have reacted if such a trial had taken place.

The late 1960s fascination with Bonnie and Clyde, brought about by

Top: Goodbye, Norma Jean is Buchanan's most successful film financially. *Bottom:* Misty Rowe stars in the title role of Buchanan's *Goodbye, Norma Jean.*

Poster art for *Goodbye, Norma Jean*.

the romanticized movie starring Faye Dunaway and Warren Beatty, gave Buchanan an angle for a film. Why not show Bonnie and Clyde as they really were? The result was a movie that cashed in at the drive-ins.

Of all his docudramas, the best is probably *Goodbye, Norma Jean.* This grim look at the early career of Marilyn Monroe isn't just a look at the difficult time she had. It seems that Buchanan was giving vent to a lot of the disgust he felt for Hollywood. The viewer can't help but be sickened by the terrible experiences young Norma Jean was forced to endure.

Goodbye, Norma Jean has been the most successful picture financially for Buchanan. It had a long run in theaters and then made the jump to television. Cable movie channels run it to this day. It's out on tape, and most rental stores have it.

Two other Buchanan films should be mentioned: *The Rebel Jesus* and *Down on Us.* Both of these films are difficult to find. *The Rebel Jesus* was shown at film festivals, winning a prize at the Atlanta festival. *Down on Us* returns to the theme of assassinations, this time of rock stars. Buchanan postulates a governmental plot to kill Janis Joplin, Jimi Hendrix, and Jim Morrison.

16

Doris Wishman: How Did a Nice Girl Like You Wind Up in a Book Like This?

She was left at loose ends. Doris Wishman, a young woman who had studied acting and worked in film distribution, was alone. She and her husband had moved to the Homestead, Florida, area in the early 1960s. Then, tragedy struck. Her husband died. Her future shaken, she had to search for something to do, something to fill her hours and provide her with a living.

Acting had been her earliest passion. She had studied at the Avalon Drama School of New York. Among her classmates was the future star Shelley Winters. Something to do with drama would be a natural for Ms. Wishman.

After drama school, she had stayed in show business, deciding on the security of a regular paycheck by working in the distribution end of the film industry. Here would be one of the most important influences on Wishman's choice of a career.

Joseph E. Levine distributed foreign films that could be picked up cheaply for the American market. He managed to come up with the rights to the infamous *Garden of Eden*, the nudist camp film that had broken down barriers of censorship in New York, Chicago, and many other major markets. *Garden of Eden* was a moneymaking machine for Levine, a fact the young Wishman had not failed to notice.

Total all this up and factor in the presence of a nudist colony nearby her home, and it all adds up to her first movie, *Nature Girl* (1962), shot at the very height of the nudist camp cycle, when several others were coming out with such fare. To make her film stand out from the rest, she needed an angle, something to pull people into the theaters.

Something turned out to be somebody. She got one of the most famous

Wishman cranked out nudist camp films one after another.

Wishman got one of the most notorious names in the striptease world for her film: Blaze Starr.

names in the striptease world, Blaze Starr, notorious for her affair with Governor Long of Louisiana. Starr's bright red hair and amazing figure would guarantee box office success.

Wishman had seen her chance and had done something with it. With a successful start behind her, she began to build a list of moneymaking credits. Movies like *Diary of a Nudist* and *Nude on the Moon* would follow.

Nude on the Moon is a particular delight taken in the context of the "space race" of the 1960s. In an era when the whole country watched as NASA built the moon program, entranced by images of men walking in space and other heroic deeds, filmmakers sought to cash in by offering a glimpse of what the moon might look like once we got there. Nobody's view was quite like Doris Wishman's.

When her astronauts landed, they discovered the moon was inhabited by nudists. Also, the place had a breathable atmosphere. The landing party could flip up the visors on their dime-store helmets and take in the whole spectacle. You can't help but sort of wish she had been right.

Critics and historians look at the release dates of Wishman's nudist films and movies she would make in other genres in later years and claim she was always behind the times. They say that is why she isn't known as widely as H. G. Lewis or Ted Mikels.

The truth is, that she wasn't behind the times. Although some nudist camp movies were coming out in the 1950s, few received any kind of distribution outside of a few burlesque houses that owned projectors. Not much money was being made in the field.

The popular view is that the nudist camp pictures were followed by the nudie-cuties, such as *The Immoral Mr. Teas*, which, in turn, were followed by the roughies, like *Scum of the Earth* and *Lorna*. In reality, things were a lot more complicated.

Court rulings won by *Garden of Eden* had made it possible to show nudist camp pictures in several cities. Attorneys had won their cases by arguing that nudism was a life-style practiced by thousands of people, who found it to be clean and healthy. The nudie-cutie was a different animal entirely. It was about voyeurism, pure and simple. It would have to fight its own court battles.

The audience wasn't nearly so discriminating. All they wanted was to see some skin. With so many markets open to nudist camp pictures, these films flourished, whereas the nudie-cuties were seen by some exhibitors and filmmakers as risky. Even Lewis and Friedman, who helped pioneer the genre with *The Adventures of Lucky Pierre*, would return to it only once, with *BOIN-N-G!* They would make at least four nudist camp pictures in the early 1960s.

Wishman waited until a genre had established itself in the exploitation field before trying it. The main reason wasn't a lack of creativity. Anyone

The Blaze Starr vehicle was released under a number of different titles.

who has seen a Wishman film would never accuse her of lacking that. It was money.

She always financed her films out of her own pocket or from loans from her family and friends. She had to make good with each project, or she might be out of filmmaking. As a result, when the first nudist camp film did well, she stuck to the genre, well after her more famous contemporaries had moved on. The movies continued to make money, and the genre itself wasn't knocked out of the skin flick market until the softcore wave of the late 1960s.

Wishman did nudist films until 1965. By then, films like Russ Meyer's *Lorna* had shown plainly that audiences were looking for new thrills. Wishman came out with her first offering in the roughies field with *Bad Girls Go to Hell*.

This is an utterly strange film that has puzzled exploitation fans ever since its release. Wishman's supporters have tried to read deep-lying themes into its story, while critics have derided it as a cheap little film gone interestingly haywire.

In the film, the lead character, a young housewife, behaves in a completely illogical manner — at least for a regular film. She goes into the hallway

As the 1960s rolled on, Wishman had to change her subject matter to keep up.

outside her apartment wearing only a see-through gown. When she is raped by the janitor, she decides she has to run away, so her husband will not know what happened. This may be a commentary on mid–1960s morality, but it doesn't make a lot of sense.

Things continue to go wrong for her. She is surrounded by strangers. She longs to talk to her husband, yet feels she can't. She is abused and miserable.

The truth may be that the deeper meaning of *Bad Girls Go to Hell* has nothing to do with any desire by Wishman to make a statement. She had to get certain elements into her film, and did so. If it made a statement, fine, as long as it got booked.

Technically, the film had some shortcomings that added to the unreality of the proceedings. The main one was that the film had been shot without sound. All the dialogue was dubbed in later. Wishman used every device she could to smooth things out, like using shots of the person who is listening in a conversation while the person talking is off camera. By doing so, she avoided having to try to post sync dialogue with lip movements.

The skin flick audience is very forgiving of such tricks as this, as long as a film delivers the goods. Many other films, such as *Naked Complex*, had done the same sort of thing; even *The Immoral Mr. Teas* was narrated. All these films showed what customers came to see, as did *Bad Girls Go to Hell*.

The thing about Wishman's films is that she went to such lengths to avoid having to do lip sync in some of them. The camera would move all about an apartment to keep from actually showing people talking. To an audience that was accustomed to seeing foreign films, with dialogue that didn't quite match lip movement, it was a strange experience.

Her reasons for shooting without sound are understandable. Often, the casts for her films would be amateurs or drawn from the world of burlesque. Few had any training as actors. On a low-budget movie, film stock is a major expense. You won't be wasting film on blown lines if you shoot silent.

Shooting silent also gave her greater freedom to move the camera. Since it didn't matter if the camera made noise, the camera didn't have to be encased in a soundproof blimp, and so it was lighter and easier to operate. Likewise, there were fewer cables to worry about and, therefore, fewer to haul about or trip over.

Shooting silent also left Wishman with one less piece of equipment to set up for each scene. That meant she could set up faster and use a smaller crew, both real money savers.

Getting her films into postproduction was a mixed bag. Editing silent footage is easier because you don't have to sync up the sound track or cut it. But silent footage has to be edited to keep the number of times you post sync with lip movement at a minimum. It forced a style upon her. Notably, some of the same elements of this style are found in the French New Wave films of the early 1960s. These directors faced the same technical problems as Wishman did. Yet they were labeled "auteurs," while Wishman, working in exploitation, has only been thought of as a curiosity.

Something needs to be said about the reported budgets of Wishman's films. Although little information exists about the early movies, the later films, like *Double Agent 73*, have been estimated to have had budgets of

Wishman returned to the striptease world for another name performer with *Deadly Weapons*.

over $200,000. This seems to be an awfully high figure for films in which a lot of corners were cut. There are a number of reasons for this high figure.

Wishman's idiosyncratic method of shooting, even when budgets allowed greater technical freedom, marked the films. But she was spending money, time, and effort, to make the films the best she possibly could. Even as early as *Nature Girl* and *Nude on the Moon*, she decided to get the best music track she could. So, she hired Doc Severinson, who would soon go on to fame on *The Tonight Show*, to orchestrate the music that her talented niece Judith had written.

She was also willing to go after cast members who had name recognition. Blaze Starr was an obvious example, in *Nature Girl*. The same film featured Ralph Young, of Sandler and Young, singers on television variety shows in the early 1960s. For *Double Agent 73* and *Deadly Weapons*, she had the 1970s most famous strip act, Chesty Morgan. Along with Morgan was the notorious Harry Reems. Known for *Deep Throat*, and all the commotion that followed it, Reems can be a surprisingly good actor when given the chance.

Wishman could spot talent, known or unknown. Her most famous find was the young Tony LoBianco, who got one of his earliest roles in Wishman's New York–set *The Sex Perils of Paulette*.

Since this reference brings us back to the 1960s, it's a good place to pick up the story of how Wishman's career progressed. In the period after *Bad Girls Go to Hell*, Wishman made films like *Another Day, Another Man* and *The Amazing Transplant*.

The *Amazing Transplant* is about a young fellow named Arthur, who admired a friend's success with the ladies. When the friend dies, Arthur has a doctor transplant his friend's sex organ to him. Rather than being successful sexually, he turns into a sex maniac and goes about attacking women. After several outrages have been committed, he turns himself in after his uncle, a policeman, convinces him that he is insane.

Wishman directed the film under the pseudonym Louis Silverman and wrote the film using Dawn Whitman as her pen name. However, not using her own name wasn't uncommon for Wishman. She actually appeared in an H. G. Lewis–Dave Friedman nudist camp picture (with her clothes on) as Doris Wisher.

Several years of roughies seemed to inspire a rebellion by Wishman in 1972, when she made *Keyholes Are for Peeping*, a throwback to the days of the nudie-cuties. Just as they were a dozen years before, the basic plot and action of this film were kept simple. A somewhat depraved janitor peeps into the rooms in his building. Any fan of the genre can imagine what he sees.

The next year would see the release of one of Wishman's best-known films, *Double Agent 73*. It would star famous ecdysiast Chesty Morgan. The

The nudie comedy *Keyholes Are for Peeping* (1972), was a throwback to the type of movie Wishman had been making ten years before.

movie's posters would claim her measurements were a ridiculous 73-32-36. Whether true or not, Ms. Morgan is very well endowed. The curious and the perverted all lined up to see this film, much like they would a traveling freak show. Although it really didn't matter what the movie was about or, for that matter, whether Ms. Morgan actually did anything or not, the resourceful Wishman came up with one of her wackiest ideas ever.

Ms. Morgan was forced to track down mobsters involved in the drug trade and do them in. After she killed them, she had to take a picture of each as proof. Did they give her a Polaroid and wish her good luck? Heck no, they implanted a camera inside her breast, one that will explode if she doesn't kill all the mobsters in a set time.

Wishman found Ms. Morgan difficult to work with and a poor actress besides. But the excellent box office persuaded Wishman to try again with her in 1980 on *Deadly Weapons*. Whereas *Double Agent 73* had been shot with sync sound, with *Deadly Weapons* Wishman returned to her favorite "mit out sound" technique.

After *Deadly Weapons*, the 1980s turned into a slow period for Wishman. Her attempt to make a comedy failed, losing her investment. Her first horror film, *A Night to Dismember*, was never released. Considering that virtually anything that could be labeled horror was making money then, it is hard to figure what happened.

These two blows almost put her out of the movie business. However, she has managed to jump back in, currently working on a direct-to-video project that she is keeping under wraps.

17

David Friedman: The Promoter

Dave Friedman is perhaps the only person in this book whose career has brought him in close contact with, or into active working relationships with, every generation of exploitation filmmaker. He knew the Forty Thieves, like the Sonney family, Dwain Esper, and Pappy Golden. He was a partner of H. G. Lewis and helped bring about the birth of the gore movie with *Blood Feast*. When exploitation turned to sexploitation, he became president of the Adult Film Association of America. But perhaps most important for Friedman was his tutelage by the biggest operator of them all, Kroger Babb.

As a young man getting out of the service, Friedman had a few dollars in his pocket and was looking for business opportunities. Just after World War II, the U. S. government had a lot of hardware on its hands that it didn't need. It takes a lot of things to fight a war besides rifles and uniforms. It takes desks, paper, nails, and hammers, and all sorts of things that a fellow might never think of; things that the government had bought tons of and now that the war was over had no need of, things like searchlights.

Friedman heard about a governmental auction that was coming up. He knew people had been grabbing all sorts of bargains at these affairs. The trouble was that the items to be auctioned were often rather odd. Who, for instance, needed huge, generator-driven searchlights?

Friedman had seen searchlights used as promotional gimmicks at everything from movie premieres to department store openings. Surely there was a market for the things.

He drove from his home in Anniston, Alabama, to the auction in Georgia. There, he bought four of the big lights and generators to power them with, paying next to nothing for these perfectly good governmental castoffs. He then placed an ad in *Boxoffice Magazine*, telling the movie world about his wonderful lights and what they would mean to anyone trying to promote a film.

A few days later, he got a call from Kroger Babb. Babb was interested in buying two of the lights if they could agree on a price. Friedman made him an offer, and after a bit of haggling, Babb said yes.

The deal did have a few conditions that Friedman would have to take care of. The first was that he would have to deliver the lights to Babb's address in Wilmington, Ohio. The second was that he would have to teach Babb how to operate the things.

To meet the first problem, Friedman rented a dilapidated old truck that looked as if it might make it to Ohio, if he had luck. He hired a black man, just out of the service, like himself, but with no chance of getting a decent job in the Alabama of the 1940s, to help him. They loaded up the crates and set out for Wilmington.

There being no interstate highway system in that day, Friedman and company were forced to wind about on state and federal roads all the way to Wilmington. It took over two days to make it. Then, when they got there, Friedman was informed that Babb wouldn't be able to meet with him until midnight.

Well, it mattered not to Friedman, as long as Babb would take the lights. They were to meet at a diner to finalize the deal. Later that night, Friedman went to wait for Babb.

That first meeting with Babb was to make a tremendous impression on Friedman. Years later, he would remember every detail of it in his autobiography *A Youth in Babylon*. Babb ordered steaks and martinis for them. They spent much of the rest of the night eating, drinking, and talking about how Babb promoted *Mom and Dad*.

Babb used the roadshow method to get his film into the theaters. But Babb's outfit was special. Other roadshow men might live the life of gypsies, rattling about the countryside in a Model T, one print of a film in the seat beside them. Not Kroger Babb. He turned roadshowing into an organized business.

He told Friedman how it all worked. Babb kept several prints of *Mom and Dad* in circulation. Each print was accompanied by an agent. This agent wasn't any ordinary type of fellow, because his duties went beyond just seeing that the film got to the theater on time and that the company got a fair count at the box office. He also had to be able to give a lecture.

As Friedman would learn, Babb promised in his advertising that the audience would receive a talk from "Eliot Forbes, America's foremost hygiene commentator." This talk was really just a spiel for a pair of $1 sex pamphlets that the audience would snap up by the hundreds. The road agent would put on his best jacket and become Eliot Forbes at each showing. After the spiel, a group of young women, dressed like nurses, would go out into the audience, selling the pamphlets.

Babb explained to Friedman the importance he placed on advertising. He sent mass mailings of circulars to every mailbox in a community where

Mom and Dad was to play. This meant thousands upon thousands of these circulars had to be printed. To cover his printing needs, Babb had his own printing plant, which turned out the circulars, as well as the sex pamphlets.

To keep track of all that was going on, Babb's office in Wilmington stayed open six days a week, keeping a small platoon of secretaries and accountants busy. Babb was the biggest fish in the exploitation pond.

Friedman liked everything that he heard and knew enough about the film business to make a favorable impression on Babb. So much so that Babb offered him a job.

But Friedman was young and independent. Though he was tempted to take the offer, he sought to carve out his own opportunities. He was the kind of fellow with the guts to do so because he still hadn't fulfilled the second part of the bargain, teaching Babb how to work the lights. He really didn't know how himself. All he had was the army manual that came with them.

Fortunately, in those days the army cared a little more about putting things into readable English than it would in later years. Friedman read the instructions and fired up the lights. It was a big success. He pocketed a substantial profit and headed back to Alabama.

It would be a while before he would see Babb or be linked to exploitation again. Soon, Friedman would become a part of one of the biggest organizations in the movie business, one that dwarfed Babb's.

Friedman went to work for Paramount Pictures. He started in the Atlanta office, learning all phases of the business, and progressed rapidly. He was particularly adept at office management. Soon, Paramount sent him to Charlotte to become the new manager there.

The offices, like the ones in Atlanta, handled all the bookings for those regions and took care of the box office receipts. Mighty Paramount never had to worry about dealing with a subdistributor, the way the smaller studios did. It had offices across the country and around the world.

Friedman had the usual problems to deal with when anyone is appointed to the top job in an office. There was jealousy because he came from another office, rather than having worked his way up in Charlotte. He dealt with the politics of the situation ably, while working wonders at organizing and motivating people. Top names in Paramount management took notice. They promoted him to the home office in New York.

Friedman's greatest interest was the publicity end of the business, and he became involved in promoting movies like *The Greatest Show on Earth*. Friedman was always able to come up with an attention-getting gimmick to draw the crowds. This skill would get him his next important assignment, to head the advertising and publicity department at the Chicago office.

It was the kind of job he had wanted all his life. Since he had visited the office of his father, a newspaper editor, and saw the publicity agents for circuses and movie companies and all types of entertainment come by, he had wanted to be a publicity man. Now, however, it had come too late.

He wanted to make it big, in a financial sense, and working for somebody else didn't seem the way to do so. Friedman decided to strike out on his own. Every fan of exploitation should be glad of his decision. At least four different types of exploitation films were influenced by Friedman. The nudist camp picture, the nudie-cutie, the gore film, and softcore sexploitation. He was also in on making what may have been the first roughie, *Scum of the Earth*. Although hardcore porno films are outside the scope of this book, his influence was certainly felt in that area, since he both made them and served as president of the Adult Filmmakers Association of America.

But moviemaking was still far in the future. For now, early in 1957, he needed a way of making a living. Being in the movie business, he had come in contact with Kroger Babb from time to time in the years since he'd sold Babb the searchlights. Babb had never lost interest in having Friedman work for him.

In Chicago, there was a special movie distributor—Modern Film Distributors. It had been formed for one purpose: to maximize the profit and cut down on unproductive competition in the "birth of a baby" film business.

At that time there were four "birth of a baby" films in circulation: *Street Corner; Because of Eve; Bob and Sally;* and the most famous of all, *Mom and Dad*. In the past, each had its own distributor. As long as these films were booked far away from each other, there was no problem. But sometimes they would be booked in theaters only a few miles apart on the same date. This type of booking had the potential of cutting the audience in half. Or, one of the films might be booked into an area just after one of the others had been shown, and the audience would already be sated (or, more likely, burned out).

Enter one organizational genius, Irwin Joseph, the owner-distributor of *Because of Eve*. Having run into situations like the ones listed, he saw the need for some sort of guiding influence over the business.

Joseph first approached Floyd Lewis, the owner of *Street Corner*. He and Lewis were friends, with offices in the same building in Chicago. Lewis agreed that a central booking office for the films was needed. Lewis had worked for Babb before going into business for himself and was still friends with his old boss. Joseph and Lewis contacted Babb, who saw the reasoning behind a central booking office and decided to join them. This left Gidney Talley, a Texan, who owned *Bob and Sally*. Babb knew him and sold him on the idea.

Since Lewis no longer had to seek bookings actively for *Street Corner*, and since he was past 70, he decided to retire. Babb was involved in other projects, and Talley's company was in Texas. So, the men decided to make Joseph the head of the company, with its Chicago offices. It had been prospering for over six years when Friedman decided to leave Paramount.

Friedman was able to step right in at Modern, becoming an independent agent for their films. Rather than receive a salary from the company, he took a percentage of each film's earnings that he booked. He was ready to go when Babb brought in a new film for Modern.

Babb called the film *Monica: The Story of a Bad Girl*. Its real name was *Sommaren Med Monica*, and it was by Ingmar Bergman. Since Harriet Andersson's bare heinie could be glimpsed in the movie, Babb saw possibilities in the art film. He chopped out whole sequences that he thought dull, threw away the score and dubbed in a new one, and dubbed English voices for the cast. Now, he was ready to put it on the road.

There was no better man to book it for him than Friedman. Friedman convinced editors of its value as an art film, pointing out the Bergman name, just becoming known in the United States. This link to Bergman won him free write-ups about the movie in the newspapers. While this was going on, he was showing the film to exhibitors, pushing the exploitable skinny-dipping shots. He booked the film throughout the Midwest, and the profits began to pour in.

Then, disaster struck. It turned out that Babb didn't own the rights to *Monica*. The film's true owner, Svensk-film, was rather hot under the collar about what seemed like Babb's theft of its film. Joseph and Friedman went to New York to try to iron things out.

Babb had bought the film from two European businessmen of good reputation, believing that they owned the rights to the film. But they had apparently been swindled by whoever it was that had sold the negative to them. Babb was left holding the bag. Not only that, he had invested a bundle in reediting, dubbing, and making prints of his version of the film.

Joseph worked his magic in the meeting with Svensk-film, realizing that Babb had a good case, not perhaps one that would stand up in court, but one that would be tied up in the legal system for years. Though it was left unsaid, both sides wanted to avoid a long court case. They struck a deal for the rights to Babb's version of *Monica*, Modern Film paying for the movie a second time, while Svensk-film was left free to sell the original to another distributor.

Of course, *Monica* wasn't the only movie Friedman was involved in booking for Modern Film. The distributor's mainstays were the "birth" movies and would remain so for as long as Modern was a going concern. It was essential that Friedman book good routes for the quartet of films.

The importance of the sex pamphlets sold at each showing of the movies is not generally known. A showing that did only fair business at the box office would make a handsome profit on the sales of these pamphlets—money that went almost entirely to Modern. Here is how it worked.

Midway in the film, the movie would stop, and "Eliot Forbes, America's foremost hygiene commentator," would take the stage, as I have already mentioned. Each of the films had its own commentator. For instance, Alexander Leeds was the pseudonym for the talker who went with *Because of Eve*.

After the pitch, when the pamphlets were sold, the talker's cut was ten cents per pamphlet. The rest went to Modern. The theater owner didn't get a penny of the pamphlet money. Those who asked for a cut got the reply, "Well, how much of your concession stand profits do we get?"

After the pitchman's ten cents was subtracted, Modern's share was almost all profit, since the pamphlets were cheaply printed at the Wilmington plant. Thus, Modern had a well-oiled, moneymaking machine.

Friedman spent most of the late 1950s booking the sex hygiene movies, often going out on the road with them. He would become a full partner in Modern Film, but it would be under sad circumstances.

Babb reached one of his life's goals when *Mom and Dad* played Broadway in 1957. There was a market for such a film in the New York area, but not as much as Babb had thought. A new era was dawning, and New Yorkers were ahead of much of the country. Sex hygiene films could play there, but they wouldn't cause the turmoil that they had in other cities, in earlier times. Babb spent heavily on advertising, but to no avail.

In fact, he spent so much that his other partners had to bail him out. In return for doing so, Babb gave up his rights to *Mom and Dad* and left Modern Film. Friedman was taken on at Modern as a partner.

The sex hygiene film, which had been the reason for Modern's existence, was in its late autumn years. The genre would have an Indian summer in 1958, largely because Friedman took the daring step of booking *Because of Eve* throughout Catholic New England. By some strange quirk, *Because of Eve* had never been rated by the Legion of Decency. Not having the C-for-condemned tag applied to it, the way *Mom and Dad* and the rest did, enabled Friedman to set up screenings in territory that had never seen a "birth" movie. The film did land-office business, filling drive-ins and selling pamphlets to an average of 50 percent of each audience.

The year 1959 would bring about some important changes for Friedman. It would see the "birth" movies begin a rapid decline that would make them unprofitable in only a short time. And it would see the beginning of a new partnership that would lift Friedman from the anonymity of film booking and promotion, where he was known within the business but not outside it, to the status of cult figure.

The reasons why the "birth" movie was fading out were plain to see, particularly to Friedman. The United States was becoming more permissive.

Books and magazines broke new ground in what could be said and shown. Hollywood films might be lagging behind literary entertainments in this respect, but a band of daring entrepreneurs out West, men like Russ Meyer and the Sonneys, were making movies of surprising boldness. The sex hygiene shows would soon be behind the times.

There was a fellow in Chicago who was just a few short years away from making history, though he didn't know it at the time. He was a Ph.D., a college-level instructor of English and creative writing. Truly a man for all seasons, he had worked in television and shot industrial films and commercials. When he came to Modern Film in 1959, it was to ask advice about making an exploitation movie. The man's name was Herschell Gordon Lewis.

Lewis told them he wanted to make the kind of movie that would make money. He wasn't out to make a statement or to create art. This nononsense approach, along with having his own financing for the film, won over Joseph and Friedman. Joseph was so enthusiastic that he decided to invest $6,000 of his own money in the venture.

Friedman and Lewis hit it off especially well. They made a deal. Friedman would teach Lewis the promotional and distribution end of the business and, in return, Lewis would teach Friedman production. The first movie they would be connected with was *The Prime Time*.

This movie, a JD picture that had Karen Black in a small role, was a learning experience for both men. Yet, perhaps not in the way they had hoped. Lewis had obtained over $100,000 from investors to make the film. For a man who would become known for his ability to put more value on the screen for each dollar spent than anybody else, it seems like a lavish budget. But for the method used to make the film, it was necessary. Lewis hadn't yet broken away from the Hollywood mind-set, shooting the movie with a full crew, buying someone else's script, and hiring a director.

Such films were usually distributed as part of a double feature. For the second half of the presentation, Friedman acquired *Carnival Story*, a Hollywood-made movie starring Anne Baxter. That film was shot in color, another selling point for getting both movies booked into drive-ins. Though four years old, the movie had never seen much of a release.

Friedman decided to premier *The Prime Time* in St. Louis, Missouri; Springfield, Illinois; and Madison, Wisconsin. He started up the publicity bandwagon and got good crowds in all three cities. Then the movie started to fizzle. Soon, it became apparent that *The Prime Time* was no money machine. It was just another JD picture at a time when there were dozens of others around.

Undaunted, Lewis pressed forward with his second feature, *Living Venus*, the story of a Hugh Hefner type who builds up his own skin magazine. Friedman took time off from booking the sex hygiene films to watch Lewis work. Lewis directed, turning out a serviceable exploitation film. Unfortunately, Modern Film was in no shape to distribute it once he got finished.

The Prime Time had used a considerable amount of Modern's resources for prints and promotional materials. Most important, it had used the time of one of its most important partners, Friedman. Its other films had won few bookings without Friedman to promote them. Lewis decided to use what he had learned from his friend to try to distribute the film himself.

This, of course, was not an easy task. Lewis struck a deal with Friedman, okayed by Modern, whereby Friedman could try to book *Living Venus* for Lewis in his spare time. This deal would lead to a meeting that would change both men's fortunes and create a legendary exploitation production unit.

As was mentioned in Chapter 4, Friedman decided to stop by the establishment of one Rose LaRose, a former stripper who owned a burlesque house in Toledo, Ohio. Friedman was going to try to book *Living Venus* in her house as the chaser film the houses would show in ten minute segments between live acts.

Miss LaRose showed little enthusiasm for *Living Venus*. What she was interested in were little ten-minute shorts that had lots of pretty, young, naked women in them. When she got those from her suppliers, she could play them forever. Unfortunately, there were so few of them around that she was stuck with playing tired old exploitation films that might show only a glimpse or two of nudity. Now, if Friedman could make some of those shorts, she would be interested.

Then and there, Friedman hatched the idea that would become *The Adventures of Lucky Pierre*. He pitched it to LaRose, who loved it. Afterward, he hurried back to Chicago, where he told Lewis.

Lewis thought they could make the film for $7,500 if they cut every corner. They brought in the long-suffering Irwin Joseph on the deal, even though *Lucky Pierre* sounded like a dirty movie to him. He told them how to set up their company financially and even put them on to an investor, Al Sack.

Sack is known mostly for his distribution, in the 1930s, 1940s, and 1950s, of films with all-black casts. These poorly made movies played theaters in black neighborhoods, making a fortune for Sack. As the 1960s dawned, these films were fading away, their stereotyped characters seen as offensive. Sack needed another kind of film to sell.

With Sack, Joseph, Lewis, and Friedman chipping in, the $7,500 was raised. Lewis went out and bought some short ends of color stock, unable to afford new rolls of film on the tiny budget. Then Friedman and Lewis began the search for a cast of nudies to populate their film.

This was not easy in Eisenhower's America. Nude models were hard

Friedman's visit to Rose LaRose would result in his classic *The Adventures of Lucky Pierre.*

to find—and pretty nude models were even harder to find. Still, they managed and even came up with a comic to play the title character. Though later they would say the cast was made up of "eight of the ugliest women ever," actually the group was attractive. Friedman searched as far away as Minneapolis for young lovelies and was able to find two at a hole-in-the-wall modeling agency he discovered. Lewis recruited from the ranks of Chicago's burlesque performers.

Friedman and Lewis wrote the script for their little film in a day. They decided that the comic who would appear in each segment for continuity would be called Lucky Pierre, named for the character in naughty rhymes they had known since their schoolboy days. Each segment would be a little adventure of his that had him coming in contact with beautiful naked women. The best of these segments, called "Drive-In Me Crazy," was about Pierre's visit to a drive-in movie.

Pierre gets in his car to go to the drive-in. He has to drive a long time to get there. Signs advertising the place start a hundred miles away. But when he finally makes it, the drive proves to be worth it. This is no ordinary establishment. They are playing *I Was a Teenage Nudist* plus *Ten Nights in a Nudist Camp.* Pierre dances for delight when he sees the marquee. But he's even more delighted when he sees the cashier. She's naked. When he drives into the lot, he is the only one there. Naked girls come out, offering popcorn for sale. He buys it as long as they keep coming. Soon, his car is jammed full of popcorn.

Then, a short subject appears on the screen. This movie within a movie is called *Picnic at the Playground.* It stars the same girls who sold Pierre the carload of popcorn. They pose on the jungle gym and merry-go-round. They also eat some sandwiches. Pierre loves it, blowing kisses at the screen.

Ad mat for *Lucky Pierre*.

Cars start to surround Pierre. First, on each side, then right behind. But, it's okay because he can still see the screen. Then, just as the main feature starts, a big step van pulls in front of him, blocking his view and wedging him in. By the time it leaves, the movies are over. The sequence ends like the others, with a pair of dice being rolled, coming up snake eyes.

Most notable about the sequence are what appear to be crane shots of Pierre's car as the other vehicles hem him in. But Friedman and Lewis didn't use a crane. They used the top of the movie screen.

Lewis had asked Friedman earlier if there was any way to climb to the peak of the screen. Friedman admitted that there was a ladder, one that went straight up inside the screen to a trap door on top. But the ledge at the top was barely three feet wide.

Lewis said he would take a camera up there and get the shot. Friedman gamely volunteered to go up with him, carrying the battery belt. With no safety rope, they crawled out onto the top of the screen, five stories above the ground, and shouted instructions with a bullhorn. They got the shots they wanted.

Until now, the story of Lewis and Friedman's films had been the same. Efficient production, but nobody wanted to play them. Now, Friedman knew he had what they wanted, and he knew the market for it. Friedman would pitch it to burlesque houses, places that had just shifted form burlesque to movies, and the most daring drive-in exhibitors. The movie caught fire immediately. Burlesque houses took in record grosses, one theater paying back almost the entire cost of the negative alone in film rental. After a bit of political horse trading with the Chicago censorship board, which Irwin Joseph took care of, they were able to book it into their hometown at the Capri theater, a real movie house, not a grind joint. The Capri was owned by Tom Dowd, a man who would be very important in Friedman's life.

The movie made an astounding $22,000 in film rental at the Capri — more than major motion pictures pulled. Friedman and Lewis were cashing in on their little movie that had been shot on short ends.

They were ready to try another, hoping for a similar payoff. Joseph told them to try a nudist camp picture. *Garden of Eden* had cleared the way for this kind of film in a lot more markets than the nudie-cuties could get into. They took his advice, starting a cycle of films that would keep them busy for the next year and a half.

The first of the group was *Daughter of the Sun,* which they decided to shoot in Florida, to mix the pleasures of a winter trip to a sunny climate with a week of profitable labor. There they met a young man, Jerry Eden, who was trying to get into films. Eden had little to offer, other than bluff and the guts to try just about anything to get his career started.

Friedman liked him. With Lewis's approval, Eden was given the role of the male lead in *Daughter*. He would work in several Friedman and Lewis productions over the next couple of years, even getting a small role in *Blood Feast*.

Friedman and Lewis needed more than just a gutsy young fellow to make a film. They needed a nudist camp that would allow them to shoot inside and, most important, an attractive female cast.

The first camp Friedman and Lewis visited made them take their clothes off before it let them in. They endured an hour of near-total embarrassment before escaping the place. Jerry Eden put them on to another camp, where the standards weren't so strict. Actually, the owner didn't care what they did in his camp, as long as they paid him. He also arranged for some "extras," a few nudists who agreed to appear in group shots for a small fee.

They needed a female lead — one who was special — so they contacted *Playboy* photographer Bunny Yeager. After checking out Friedman and Lewis to make sure they were on the up and up, Yeager put them in touch with one of her models, Rusty Allen.

Much to their delight, Ms. Allen was beautiful. She couldn't act, but that really wasn't a requirement for this kind of picture. Lewis was willing to rewrite her lines, so they could be spoken by a narrator.

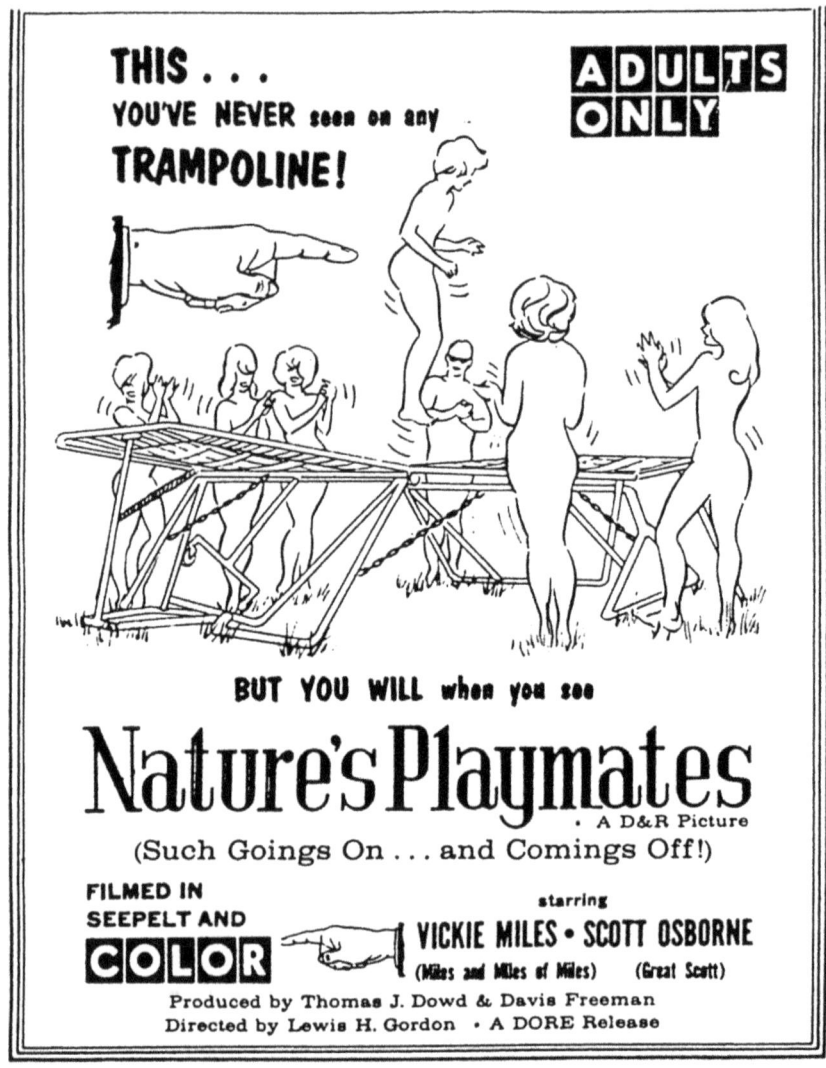

Tiring of volleyball, Friedman and Lewis hit on the idea of using a trampoline.

If they had an worries, it was with her escort. He was a greasy sort, the leather jacketed hoodlum type of that time. He came with her to their first meeting with Friedman and Lewis. They couldn't believe that such a doll was going around with that kind of guy. Afterward, Friedman got an even bigger surprise. It turned out that her escort wasn't a hoodlum. Her escort wasn't even a man. Ms. Allen was a lesbian. This didn't bother Friedman a bit. They went right ahead and shot their film.

Nature's Playmates capitalized on the Twist dance craze.

With more markets to play in, *Daughter of the Sun* became an even bigger hit than *The Adventures of Lucky Pierre*. Friedman and Lewis were drawing a lot of attention in the world of exploitation, particularly from their favorite theater owner, Tom Dowd.

Dowd wanted to get into the nudist film business himself. Rather than risk jumping in alone, having no production experience, he hired Friedman and Lewis to make a movie for him. This film was *Nature's Playmates*.

The film would be a detective story. Dowd wanted more plot in his film than the general run of such pictures. So, Friedman told Lewis, who took to his typewriter and wrote the first nudist noir, as some have called it.

In the movie, a man has run away from his wife. She hires two detectives, a man and woman, who trace him to a Florida nudist camp. On questioning, the man reveals his true reason for leaving his wife: He is totally committed to the nudist life-style, but his wife would never try it. The detectives persuade her to try nudism. She likes it, and so do the detectives. They fall in love and decide to get married.

Playing the female detective was Allison Louise Downe, who would go on to become a permanent member of the Friedman and Lewis team. When the troupe returned to Chicago, Downe was with them. She would act in several of the pair's films and serve in every production capacity, from typist to makeup artist.

Dowd was happy with the picture. It was far ahead of most other offerings, particularly in telling a story. Most other nudist films hadn't gone beyond the standard "fuddy-duddy gets won over to nudism" plot. Although *Nature's Playmates* depended on this old ploy for its ending, it was different enough to influence other makers of such fare, who now would have to have better stories to keep up.

None would be quite so unusual as the next idea Dowd brought to

Ad mat for *Nature's Playmates*.

Friedman. Dowd wanted to call it *Singing in the Sun*. It would be the first nudie musical.

On their previous trip to Florida, a piano player in a Miami bar pitched Dowd a movie script and some songs. Dowd was somewhat soused that evening. But even when he sobered up, Dowd felt enthusiastic about the idea. So much so, that he bought the package and even signed up the piano player's boy wonder singer, Rex Marlowe.

Friedman was appalled. When he heard Marlowe sing, he felt even worse. Then Dowd gave him the fine piece of news that he wanted to shoot the film in Florida during the last two weeks of August. It was a demented idea. An awful tenor running around naked in the August heat, singing execrable songs. Naturally, Friedman said to count him and Lewis in.

Dowd wanted to spend some real money on this one. He rented a yacht and a nightclub as locations. The yacht sequence was nearly a disaster. When a little old lady next door to where the boat was tied up looked out and saw a yard full of naked people, she called the cops. Friedman had to do some fast explaining, but managed to smooth things out. Nobody went to jail, and they were able to go back to filming, as soon as they rounded up the cast, who had taken to the hills.

The film would be released as *Goldilocks and the Three Bares*. Friedman and Lewis managed to turn an amateur script into a decently made little movie. Like the other nudies they shot, it raked in the dough for Tom Dowd. The Friedman and Lewis team had taken their fee up front, hired to do the job, the way they had been on *Nature's Playmates*.

All this moviemaking for other producers had Friedman and Lewis hungry to make a film of their own—one that if it made a profit, would make that profit for them. Having been in the nudie business for a while, they had seen quite a bit that was funny in the genre. They decided to make the nudie-comedy *BOIN-N-G!*

BOIN-N-G! was the slightly autobiographical story of two guys who decide to make a nudie film. Never mind that they have never made a film before or even that they have no real idea of what it takes to make one. They figure that anybody could make a picture as good as the ones they've been seeing at the local exploitation cinema.

They search diligently for cameras, film stock, and the hardest commodity to find—female cast members who are willing to disrobe. One of the guys, an ad man, finds that his secretary wants to be in the picture. This scene had a parallel in real life, since Bunny Downe, the Friedman and Lewis team's Jill-of-all-trades, would appear in the film.

They finally gather a cast and go to the countryside to film. There, they are joined by their cameraman, Schmurtz. Schmurtz talks a good game, pretending to know big stars by their first names. Our two heroes follow his rather doubtful advice, even though Schmurtz doesn't know enough to check to see if the camera is loaded with film.

Their movie finished, they stuff it into grocery bags and head out to show it to a distributor. The film is so bad that our heroes sink beneath their seats as it unspools. The distributor declares, "This is the worst movie I've ever seen. I'll buy it."

BOIN-N-G! was the first film that Lewis and Friedman shot in their new partnership with drive-in owner Stan Kohlberg. The deal they made was for Kohlberg to bankroll the pictures, while Friedman and Lewis provided all the production skills and equipment. After the films were completed, Friedman would be in charge of distributing them. Other than signing his name on the checks, Kohlberg might show up to have his picture taken for publicity purposes. Otherwise, he stayed out of the way.

Late in the fall of 1962, Friedman and Lewis were ready to go again, even though they had just finished *BOIN-N-G!* in September. The movie would be about a smut racket and would be shot in Florida, getting them out of the November chill for a week. Friedman pitched the idea to Kohlberg, who was enthusiastic. He gave them the money, and they set out.

Perhaps the best thing about the new movie was its title, *Scum of the Earth*. This film is probably the first of the "roughies" genre, beating out Russ Meyer's *Lorna* by about a year. However, all the roughies were preceded by films like *Kiss Me Deadly*, the adaptation of Mickey Spillane's novel, and others that depended on sleaze and violence with sex to draw a crowd.

Scum of the Earth was certainly a switch from *BOIN-N-G!* Perhaps now it doesn't seem so strange that the makers of a movie like *Blood Feast* would produce *Scum of the Earth*. But the change in tone, from the naughty, but

funny *BOIN-N-G!* to this hard-edged, at times depressing, film signaled a turning point in their careers.

They were ready to make history, but, of course, they had no inkling of it at the time. They only knew that a friend of Friedman's, Eli Jackson, wanted them to make a film for him. It would be another nudist camp epic, with Jackson's wife, burlesque queen Virginia Bell, as its star. Since they would be going to Florida to shoot it, they figured they could stay an extra week and shoot a film of their own. This film would be *Blood Feast.*

Miami now brings to mind retirement homes, Little Havana, and the world of "Miami Vice." But in February 1963 it was a much different place — a strip of hotels and motels along the beach and a friendly downtown section. It wasn't really a city. It was just a good-sized town that made most of its money from tourism.

One of the motels along the beach was the Suez. Friedman and Lewis would stay there, along with their cast and crew, every time they made a film in Miami. The owner loved having them. Whenever they were shooting a scene at the motel, the owner would invite the other guests to watch. That is, when it wasn't a nude scene. Friedman and Lewis didn't mind the crowd. As part of the deal, the owner would let them shoot in an empty room, rent free, when they needed it.

Friedman and the gang finished *Bell, Bare and Beautiful* in only four days. Now, they were ready to start on their own film. They began to gather some strange props — things that probably no one had thought of putting in a movie before.

Things like sheep entrails, brains, and a tongue. They got eyeballs, and a leg from a department store mannequin. At a cosmetics lab they went hunting for stage blood — not just a little; they needed gallons of it. And this stage blood would have to look real enough to convince a movie audience. They planned to shoot a lot of close-ups.

With their crude special effects department well stocked, they proceeded to shoot the ultimate Halloween show of its time, the movie that would gag a nation.

It started with Sandy Sinclair, who had been in *Scum of the Earth.* She is taking a bubble bath, when in comes the demented Egyptian caterer, Faud Ramses, his mind set on preparing "the most horrendous of all feasts," as the ads would proclaim. Faud stabs Ms. Sinclair's character to death, then carves off a leg and takes out an eyeball and tosses them in his sack.

The slaughter well under way, we are treated to the sight of the Great Pyramid and the Sphinx. This shot for the title sequence used a miniature Great Pyramid and Sphinx that sat in front of the Suez Motel. It was free, and it was there, so why not?

Opposite: **Pages from the comic book used to promote** *Scum of the Earth.*

The audience was never allowed to regain its balance. Soon, Faud was at work again. Though the acting was atrocious, audiences were so busy cringing from the gore that they hardly noticed the acting.

It's a good thing. Mal Arnold, as Faud Ramses; Connie Mason, as Suzette Freemont; and Lyn Boulton, as Suzette's mother, make up one of the most untalented casts in motion picture history. Only William Kerwin (using his Thomas Wood screen name), as the policeman, and Scott Hall, as his boss, gave credible performances. Scott Hall, it should be remembered, traveled about the country with Kroger Babb's *Mom and Dad*, hawking pamphlets as "Eliot Forbes, America's foremost hygiene commentator." Friedman had called his friend down from his Sarasota home to be in the picture.

Kerwin was making one of his frequent appearances in a Friedman and Lewis production. He had played Virginia Bell's suitor in *Bell, Bare and Beautiful* and stayed on to act in his best-known role. Another Friedman and Lewis regular, Jerry Eden, would play the role of an ancient priest who sacrifices a virgin, cutting her heart out.

Though many figures have been given for *Blood Feast*'s budget, the check Kohlberg wrote to cover it all was for $24,500. The film would eventually make over $4 million at the box office, in a day when many drive-ins charged 50 cents for admission.

Blood Feast was an instant hit. The money came flowing into Kohlberg's office. Soon, he was urging the pair of filmmakers to make another.

Friedman told Lewis, who was ready to go. But this time Lewis wanted to do something better. *Blood Feast* had been shot from a 14-page script, a document that was hardly better than an outline. Their main objective had been to show violence in a realistic fashion, story a secondary consideration, just as with the nudies. Lewis wanted to do it right this time. He wanted a strong story that would play on people's fears and deliver real shocks. He wanted to stay a step ahead of the audience, realizing that special effects alone might not get the job done the second time around.

Lewis told Friedman that it would cost a big piece of change to do the kind of movie he wanted to—in the neighborhood of $60,000. This would be the biggest budget since *Living Venus*, which had been shot with a union crew.

Friedman took the news back to Kohlberg. The best indication of how much money *Blood Feast* was making was that Kohlberg didn't bat an eye at the figure. He told them to go ahead.

Friedman and Lewis journeyed to the peaceful little town of St. Cloud, Florida. Here, Friedman was truly in his element, like a circus owner bringing the show to town. Except that this time, everybody in town would get to be a part of the show. Friedman had people turning out in droves for the chance to be extras in a crowd scene.

The movie, *Two Thousand Maniacs,* was about a town that had been destroyed by Union soldiers during the Civil War. Now, a hundred years later, it had come back to life to seek revenge on a group of Yankee tourists.

The story had a couple of things going for it, since the centennial of the Civil War's end was coming up, and books, magazines, and television, were full of Civil War stories. Also, there was a certain fear among Northerners of what could happen to you if you got off the main roads while passing through the South. The image of revenge-crazed rednecks seemed quite real to some people.

Friedman and Lewis got a decent cast together. William Kerwin was back to play one of the leads, as was Connie Mason. Mason, a former *Playboy* playmate, had apparently taken some acting lessons in the interval between films. In *Blood Feast,* she read all her lines off cue cards and could be seen doing it. She seemed to tighten up every time the camera was pointed in her direction. But in *Two Thousand Maniacs,* her delivery had smoothed out. She was learning to relax and to respond to the other characters' lines.

In a supporting role, Jeffrey Allen was in fine form as the mayor. The part of Bea, who has her thumb cut off by one of the rednecks, was played by Shelby Livingston. And all those appearances in the nudies and the nonspeaking part in *Blood Feast* finally paid off for Jerry Eden. He got the part of John, Bea's husband. He was the one fellow the audience wanted to see the maniacs get.

Another notable part of the film was its music. Lewis wrote an original bluegrass score, played by the Pleasant Valley Boys. The band would appear from time to time as a kind of Greek chorus. Somehow, the gentle melodies of bluegrass took on a sinister feel. It was the best score ever in a Friedman and Lewis picture.

Friedman's mark on the picture came from his love of carnivals and the midway. He devised a game that the rednecks would play with one of their tourist victims. It was similar to the old-fashioned dunking tank, except that the victim didn't get dunked. A boulder fell on him and smashed him flat.

The extra money they spent turned *Two Thousand Maniacs* into the most polished production the team had ever done. It looked like they had spent five times the money. Unfortunately, this extra effort didn't pay off at the box office.

Two Thousand Maniacs never got the chance it deserved because of the trouble *Blood Feast* had stirred up. It has often been said that *Blood Feast* slipped by the censorship boards, but that the boards were ready and waiting when *Two Thousand Maniacs* came along. *Maniacs* never got the playdates that *Blood Feast* did. Where it did play, like in Southern drive-ins, it did great business.

Gore, for a while, was near a stopping place, at least partly because these are two of the most undefendable films ever made. (That's probably why exploitation fans like them so well. An "over the top" effort will win them every time.) The last film of the "gore trilogy" was about to be made.

Color Me Blood Red didn't get the kind of budget that *Maniacs* got. With fewer theaters willing to book their grisly entertainments, Friedman and Lewis were willing to cut back their expenditures accordingly. Since Kohlberg had to clear all he had invested before Friedman and Lewis saw so much as a penny for their labors, it's easy to understand why they were ready to make a smaller film this time.

The gore was also somewhat restrained. Still, there was plenty of Barfred stage blood on hand, and it would play the key part in the story. A painter, played by Adam Sorg, has been ignored for years. But when some blood gets mixed in with his paint, the canvases draw raves from the critics. To maintain his lofty position, he has to have a steady supply of human blood.

The movie is surprisingly effective, mostly because of Sorg's performance. He may chew the scenery from time to time, but it works.

Something that wasn't working was the relationship between Friedman and Lewis. Near the end of production, they had an argument. Some accounts say that it was over money. Others say it was about how the film was being shot. At any rate, one of the most productive partnerships in exploitation filmmaking was coming to an end.

Each had filled a need in the partnership. Friedman knew campaigns and distribution, Lewis knew writing and production. Each taught the other until, finally, each knew about as much as the other did. Now, each had to test the waters alone.

The split also ended Lewis's partnership with Kohlberg. Later, Lewis would have to go to court to try to get his share of the profits from *Blood Feast*. The courts turned him down. He was never able to receive what was owed him.

Kohlberg's relationship with Friedman was a little better, but only slightly. Friedman was ready to try his luck on the West Coast. This would leave Kohlberg with *Color Me Blood Red* unedited and unreleasable.

Friedman found an editor who would put together the film. He also decided to sell all his rights to *Blood Feast* and the other pictures he had made in partnership with Kohlberg to Kohlberg. This would give him the kind of cash he needed to set himself up in Los Angeles. He sold his rights to *Lucky Pierre* and *Daughter of the Sun* to Lewis. Now, his ties to Chicago were broken.

Out in Hollywood he set up a deal with Dan Sonney, who had distributed *Blood Feast* and *Two Thousand Maniacs* in the West. Friedman

Friedman's first film after breaking with Lewis was *The Defilers*.

started his own company, Entertainment Ventures, with offices in Sonney's building. His company's first film would be *The Defilers*.

Friedman recruited sexploitation director Lee Frost to interpret the script for him. The film draws its inspiration from a John Fowles story, *The Collector*. Friedman changed elements of the story about, having two young men, instead of just one man, kidnap the woman.

Going along with the trend, Friedman shot this roughie in black and white, as most other producers of such fare were doing at that time. It gave it a gritty feel. This, along with Frost's surprisingly effective direction, made *The Defilers* a winner for Friedman.

He would follow this success with such efforts as *A Smell of Honey, A Swallow of Brine!* which had Laszlo Kovacs as the cameraman, and *The Notorious Daughter of Fanny Hill*. These films in the mid-1960s would lead up to one of his biggest drive-in hits, released in 1969, *Starlet*.

Friedman made a satire on *Valley of the Dolls* and on the nudie business itself. He used his own company, EVI, as the backdrop for the film and even appeared in it briefly as himself.

Starlet is the story of three young women in Hollywood, who are roommates. The film starts with one of the girls, Carol, making a stag film. Rick, the guy in the stag, tells her before they do a shot, "I'll be gentle."

Carol says, "Be obscene, and not heard."

Starlet is peppered with this kind of wisecracking. We have Friedman himself to thank for it. He came up with the story idea and did the screenplay himself. By the looks of things, he had a great deal of fun doing it. There are a number of in-jokes. For instance, when they start to slate a scene in one of the films they're making, the clapper board lists the cameraman as Lewis. Sort of like saying, "Hi, there!" to his old partner.

There are a number of subplots in the movie. One of the roommates' boyfriends gets a chance to direct a nudie at EVI. It turns out that this nudie will be about the Pilgrims! One day on a set, they're shooting a biker movie, the next day, on the same set, they put up a set of stocks, so the S&M crazed Pilgrims can have at it. Nothing was too outrageous for Friedman to put in this film.

It should be noted that Friedman used several different sets for his film, and all of them are top notch. There's even a western street scene, where a shootout it staged. The pictures Friedman was making at this point in his career were far ahead of the competition. They looked better than most television shows of the time and as good as many studio films. Friedman made use of the larger pool of talent available to him in Hollywood, getting a cast that could really act.

In *Starlet*, EVI is going to make a "big" movie, *A Youth in Babylon*. Friedman evidently liked that title. Twenty years later, he would use the title for the first volume of his autobiography.

Soon, the film world would change. Softcore films were knocked out of the market by hardcore pornos. Friedman didn't like the hardcore films, but wound up making them anyway, trying, and succeeding, in making a good-quality product. These films, outside the scope of this book, should be listed anyway. Friedman produced *Seven into Snowy*, *Chorus Call*, and *Matinee Idol*. During this period, he became president of the Adult Film Association of America, a position he held for 17 years.

He is currently retired and living in Anniston, Alabama.

18

Rogues' Gallery: A Cast of Dozens

In the period this book covers, roughly from the 1920s to the present, hundreds of exploitation films have been made. Trying to include all the makers of such fare in this book would be impossible for a variety of reasons other than the most obvious, that one volume couldn't hold so many chapters.

Some of the filmmakers' careers are still shrouded in mystery. A few of them want it that way, preferring not to be known as the makers of blood-and-guts movies or as the purveyors of smutty little black-and-white skin flicks. Others have simply been ignored, and now their stories are in danger of being lost, as they and their contemporaries age and finally go to the big drive-in in the sky.

Some filmmakers had only one shot at glory, and failed, but did so in such a remarkable fashion that they should not be left in obscurity. Many had terrible distribution that left them little more than legendary figures to exploitation fans, who, even with video, have yet to see their films. This chapter draws names from all of these categories and throws in a few surprises.

Max Baer, Jr.: As you have already guessed, he is one of the surprises. Forever stigmatized by his role as Jethro on "The Beverly Hillbillies," Baer didn't have a lot of career options open to him after the series went off the air. He had played the role of Jethro too well, for too long. People actually thought he was like the bumbling oaf he played.

Perhaps he decided to go along with them. In a move reminiscent of Jethro's screen persona, Beef Jerky, Baer decided to produce and act in his own film. It would be the 1974 drive-in hit, *Macon County Line*.

Shot on a budget of $250,000, the film would bring in over $12 million. Baer's portrayal of the sheriff, who pursues the innocent teenagers he suspects of committing a series of crimes, is convincingly evil. Suddenly, Max Baer was a name to be reckoned with at the box office.

Two years later, Baer was ready to try his luck again. Since his greatest success had been on the Southern drive-in circuit, he decided to tailor a film to meet the audience. This would result in *Ode to Billy Joe*.

Baer took the 1967 country-western hit song by Bobbie Gentry as the basis for his film. If you ever wondered why Billy Joe jumped off the Talahatchee Bridge, this film explains it all. If you don't mind my spoiling the surprise, Billy Joe's guilt over a gay sexual experience drives him to jump.

Maybe it was this element, or that the movie gets off to a fairly slow start, that prevented it from performing up to expectations at the drive-ins, though it did do reasonably well.

In 1979, Baer would try one more time. *Hometown USA* was a rather raunchy version of *American Graffiti*. It was close enough, in plot, if not in tone, to create some controversy. Accusations of plagiarism worked against the film ever being booked widely. The film should have been successful. It would have fit right in with the wave of teenage sex comedies that hit in the early 1980s. Perhaps it was just a little before its time.

Ed Wood: He may be the best known of all the filmmakers in this book, but for all the wrong reasons. In their Golden Turkey Awards, the Medved brothers named him the worst director of all time and his *Plan 9 from Outer Space*, the worst movie ever.

Actually, there are far worse films out there than *Plan 9*, and worse directors than Ed Wood. Wood simply was a fellow without much talent and utterly no money. As exploitation films go, he was a minor figure, his movies never making much money, at least for him. It was only after his death and the beginning of the bad movie craze that others cashed in on his work.

Wood made films in several different genres. He was assistant director and production manager on *The Lawless Rider,* a western that went disastrously over its $17,500 budget. He made the remarkably daring, for its time, *Glen or Glenda,* a story about transvestites and transsexuals. (Yes, it is loaded with stock footage, and the dream sequences look ridiculous, but he made this film in 1953. It took a lot of guts to tackle such a subject then.) There was horror/science fiction like *Bride of the Monster* in his repertoire and crime films like *Jailbait*.

He worked as a scriptwriter only on *The Violent Years,* a story about a gang of teenage girls who commit crimes for kicks. Later in his career, he scripted *Orgy of the Dead,* an excuse to show a bunch of striptease acts. For sheer weirdness, there is nothing else in the nudie field to beat it. It has the spirits of the dead, strippers, doing their acts in a graveyard, while the Devil, played by Criswell, looks on.

A. C. Stephen, whose real name was Stephen Apostoloff, directed this masterpiece. He and Wood would be back together for *Fugitive Girls,* a sexed-up remake of Wood's *The Violent Years*.

William C. Thompson: Any discussion of Wood brings to mind his cinematographer. Many ill-informed people see Thompson's name in the *Plan 9* credits and think of the day-for-night fiasco, blaming him for it.

This is the well-known scene where Bela Lugosi's stand in strides through the graveyard, late at night, to menace the stranded girl. In the next shot, a fat guy in a cowboy hat rescues her. The trouble was, that shot was in broad daylight. Then, we cut back to the Lugosi stand in, and it's night.

Obviously, the lab was supposed to print the rescue shot day for night, and somehow goofed. This wasn't Thompson's fault. *Plan 9* was shot on such a miniscule budget that nothing could be done about it once the error was discovered.

Miniscule budgets were nothing new to Thompson. He was cameraman cinematographer on some of the lowest of low-budget Hollywood exploitation films. If you had a few thousand dollars to cobble together a feature with and couldn't do the camera work yourself, you sent for Thompson. He made surprisingly good efforts on some of the worst films ever made that were often the only factor that saved them from total amateurism.

Dwain Esper's *Maniac* may be a case in point. The actors were hammy, Esper just wanted a film he could roadshow, but Thompson turned in a professional effort on the pennies he had to work with.

When given a chance with a good director, Thompson did memorable work. The best evidence of this is *Daughter of Horror*, a noir tale of madness. This 1953 attempt to step inside the mind of an insane woman on the night that his madness reaches its peak is one of the most unusual films from the period. Unfortunately, it probably was a bit too unusual, never really finding an audience until video came along. Its director, a very talented fellow by the name of John Parker, never got another chance to direct.

Steve Hawkes: A true one-shot wonder. *Blood Freak* is his only known film, and this is a tragedy because there's no telling what kind of loony career he might have had if *Blood Freak* had somehow caught on.

If that title sounds a little close to Herschell Gordon Lewis's *Blood Feast*, there's a reason for it. Hawkes apparently idolized Lewis as a filmmaker and did so a long time before it became fashionable. His *Blood Freak* was filmed in 1972. Hawkes also played the lead character, Herschell, in the film.

When we first see Hawkes in the film, we realize he had one other hero in his life who was the equal of Lewis. It was Elvis Presley. Yes, Hawkes was a real trailblazer. Not only was he a Lewis fan before that was acceptable, he was an Elvis impersonator at a time when nobody even thought of it.

William C. Thompson's best work appeared in *Daughter of Horror*.

One can only speculate on this fellow's teenage years, growing up following two of the 1960s icons. Perhaps he listened to his Elvis records by day, then bopped over to the drive-in for *Two Thousand Maniacs* at night. Or, maybe a wild double feature of *Love Me Tender* and *Color Me Blood Red* warped his mind forever. Whatever sent him down this strange path, I'm glad it did.

The action starts with one of the most inept tracking shots ever committed to film. Herschell/Hawkes is cruising down the highway on his motorcycle. Apparently he was after the type of shot seen so frequently in biker movies of the time, where the cameraman rides ahead of the biker, shooting out of the back of a pickup truck. The trouble was, the road was a bit bumpy. The camera was bouncing all over the place, sometimes almost losing Herschell completely.

The plot, in a nutshell is this: Herschell becomes a pot addict. At the poultry farm where he works, he eats a turkey that has been fed an experimental drug to make it grow faster. The pot and the drug-laced bird combine in his system, turning him into a blood-crazed turkey monster.

No, I'm not making this up. And it gets better. One fellow has his leg cut off by the turkey monster, who accomplishes his evil deed with a radial arm saw. It is very graphic, just like goremeister Lewis would have done it. But the most interesting thing about it all is that we see the victim walking about a good bit before he gets done in, and he is already walking with a limp. Did Hawkes hire a one legged man for this ghastly effect?

At any rate, the turkey monster episode turns out to be a pot-induced hallucination, Herschell becomes a born-again Christian, and the whole thing is one of the most wonderfully demented films ever made.

William Kerwin: Kerwin is best known for his appearances in the films of H. G. Lewis, particularly as the policeman in *Blood Feast* and as one of only two survivors of the group of tourists beset by *Two Thousand Maniacs*. He acted in at least 11 films for Lewis from 1960 to 1967 and held crew positions, often uncredited, on others. Whenever Lewis wanted to make a film, Kerwin was ready to lend a hand.

His first role in a Lewis film was as the publisher of a girlie magazine, in *Living Venus*. He auditioned for the role, bringing along a short film he had done for the Catholic church. This film was an earnest attempt to draw young men to a career in the priesthood. I've often wondered what the church thought when its spokesman turned up playing a Hugh Hefner type in a movie about the skin mag racket.

Living Venus was a union-made picture, so Kerwin used his own name. But the team of Lewis and Friedman temporarily fell on hard times. Their scramble for work led to the nudie-cutie classic *Lucky Pierre*, which not only was shot without union participation, but had only a three-man crew. This film led to more work for Kerwin, and a name change as well.

Since he was listed in the Screw Actors Guild as William Kerwin, he had to use an alias on this shoot so he would not get in trouble. He used the name Thomas Sweetwood, playing the small part of a fellow who hires Pierre to do some plumbing for him. Pierre does the work, while the man's wife is taking a bath right beside him. Kerwin played his bit and doubled as the third man on the crew, being the gofer for cameraman Lewis and soundman Friedman.

The year 1963 was a bumper one for Lewis and Friedman, as well as for William Kerwin. Kerwin would star as a first-time filmmaker in the nudie-cutie *BOIN-N-G!* again using the name Thomas Sweetwood. This film would be followed by the nudist camp musical, *Goldilocks and the Three Bares*. In *Scum of the Earth*, he was a sleazy photographer, who turned good guy by the end of the picture. Then would come the trip to Florida that would gain him roles in two features and a claim to fame.

The trip didn't get off to an auspicious start. Kerwin had agreed to help drive Lewis's van straight through to Florida. They actually got there ahead of Lewis and Friedman, having to wait in the parking lot at the Suez Motel because the owner wouldn't let them into their rooms until Lewis showed up to okay it. So, after their marathon drive, they got to bake in the parking lot until the boss men arrived, having journeyed by plane.

Then, Eli Jackson showed up. He was the producer of the first film they would make, *Bell, Bare and Beautiful*. He demanded that they start shooting at ten o'clock that night, even though nobody had seen the script. Game for anything, Kerwin learned his lines, doing his best with the amateur writing.

With that film polished off, Kerwin was ready to act in the first hardcore gore movie, *Blood Feast*. He would also undergo another name change, casting aside his nom de nudie, Sweetwood, for the tougher sounding Thomas Wood.

As in many of the other pictures he had done for Lewis and Friedman up to this point, he was one of the only competent actors in the cast. But then, nobody was going for art with this picture. It was a kind of gross practical joke. He waded through gallons of Barfred stage blood in pursuit of the demented Egyptian Faud Ramses, on his way to another starring role, 1964's *Two Thousand Maniacs*.

Though it didn't get the attention that *Blood Feast* did, *Maniacs* is far the better picture. When surrounded with better talent and given a genuinely frightening script to work with, Kerwin rose to the occasion, giving one of his best performances.

Kerwin would never have as busy a period again in his career. He missed out on the last of the gore trilogy, *Color Me Blood Red*, though he would do a version of the mad artist story several years later.

In 1966 he was in Lewis's *An Eye for an Eye*, the story of a blind man who receives an eye transplant. When his bandages are removed, he can see the very last thing the donor saw before he was killed, the man who murdered him. Unfortunately, the film had practically no release and is not available on video.

Things picked up in 1967. Kerwin had a part in Lewis's "wife swapping" story, *Suburban Roulette*. He appeared for the last time in a Lewis movie in *A Taste of Blood*, playing the role of Dr. Tyson, who comes to realize that his best friend is a vampire.

Kerwin's most notable film in the post–Lewis phase of his career was *Playgirl Killer*, directed by Erick Santamaria, the mad artist story mentioned earlier. Kerwin plays an artist who cannot stand the distraction of having his models move. So, he kills them and freezes them in place in a meat locker.

Kerwin moved to Miami and started acting under the name Rooney Kerwin. He died in 1989.

Arch Hall, Sr.: He was a test pilot who made nudie films, a fellow with more schemes than there were hours of the day to hatch them in. He made some of the campiest films of the early 1960s, at a time when a bumper crop of such movies was coming along. He's the kind of fellow you say to yourself, "They ought to write a book about this guy," and the thing is, somebody already has.

If you've read the book or seen the movie *The Last Time I Saw Archie*, then you know a bit about the kind of person Arch Hall was. Bill Bowers used him as a character in his novel. Everyone who knew Hall says that Bowers really captured him; however, like all novels, it is a work of fiction and not really an account of Hall's life. The movie made from it is excellent, starring Robert Mitchum as Archie.

But neither the movie nor the book tells about Hall's second career, that of filmmaker. He climbed on the nudie bandwagon in the early 1960s, making films like *Magic Spectacles* and *What's Up Front*. The former movie's title pretty well sums up the plot. The wearer of said spectacles got to see ladies without their clothes, and not much more of an excuse was needed for crafting a nudie flick. *What's Up Front* was about the adventures of a bra salesman. It starred Marilyn Manning, a former exotic dancer.

These two films alone would not have won him a place in the hearts of exploitation fans. It would take the films he made later, starring his son, Arch Hall, Jr., to make his reputation.

For his Fairway International company, Hall produced such star vehicles as *The Choppers* for his son. It was about a gang of teenage car thieves. It did well in the drive-in market it was intended for. Hall followed it with the cult favorite *Eegah!*

This story of a love-sick caveman featured several of Hall's regular stock company. Of course, there was Arch, Jr., as well as Marilyn Manning

Ruggero Deodato proved with *The Last Survivor* that he is a master filmmaker.

and Hall himself, acting under the name William Watters. He directed as well, using Nicholas Merriwether as his alias.

But the most memorable performance was by the title character, Eegah, played by Richard Kiel. Legend has it that the seven-foot-tall Kiel owed Hall rent for an apartment Hall was letting Kiel have. With no way of getting the money out of the nearly penniless Kiel, Hall had him act in *Eegah!*

Hall gave another cult favorite his first big chance. He hired Ray Dennis Steckler to direct *Wild Guitar*. Steckler had worked on the crew of *Eegah!* and knew what it took to get a film in the can for almost nothing, which was what their budget was for this movie. Both Steckler and Hall joined Arch, Jr., in the cast of this movie about the recording business.

Perhaps the best movie Hall ever took part in was *The Sadist*. He produced it, turning over the director's job to James Landis. In the movie, Arch, Jr., plays a psycho terrorizing three schoolteachers stranded at a junkyard in the desert. It sustains tension and has a few real jolts in it.

Arch, Jr., wasn't really interested in the movie business. When he decided to quit, Arch, Sr., decided to give it up as well, ending one of the more remarkable careers in the exploitation game.

Ruggero Deodato: This man is responsible for a pair of the most powerful and, some would say, most revolting films ever to appear on a movie screen. They are *The Last Cannibal World* and *Cannibal Holocaust*. A viewing of either of these movies is one of the most intense experiences the VCR can provide.

It isn't just the effects, which are well done, or the subject matter that gives the films their punch. Deodato is a filmmaker of the caliber of Tobe Hooper on *The Texas Chainsaw Massacre*. He knows what he is doing and doesn't back off an inch. Both films are extremely well made, without being Hollywood slick. This adds to their dreadful reality.

Deodato got his break in films from what seems like an unlikely source. Roberto Rossellini hired him as his second assistant. Deodato got the job mainly because he happened to live in the same apartment building as Rossellini and had been a friend of Rossellini's son.

A second assistant on an Italian film is a sort of educated gofer. He has to have knowledge of how films are made, but doesn't need to have any experience. Deodato got the experience he needed with Rossellini, working on two as a second assistant, then doing five more as first assistant director, before striking out on his own.

His first assignment as director was *Live Like a Cop, Die Like a Man*, which followed with *Concorde Affair*, and *Last Feelings*, a romance movie. None of these films sounds like the background of a fellow who would make movies about cannibalism. Remember though that Tobe Hooper made *Eggshells* before he made *The Texas Chainsaw Massacre*.

What started Deodato down the path to cinematic chills, controversy, and even trouble with the law was a magazine article. It was the story of a man who had been captured by a primitive tribe, the Rock People, and held as their prisoner. This true story took root in Deodato's imagination, finally coming to the screen as *The Last Cannibal World*.

Released in the United States under a variety of titles (*Cannibal, Jungle Holocaust*, and *The Last Survivor*), it is the most gripping of Deodato's pair of cannibal films. Though *Cannibal Holocaust* may surpass it in sheer savagery, the audience's identification with the man captured by the cannibals is so strong that the suspense reaches almost unbearable levels.

Whereas *The Last Cannibal World* was meant simply to tell a story, *Cannibal Holocaust* was made for a different reason. Deodato saw the violence in the world about him, the kidnapping and murder of Aldo Moro by the Red Brigades and other acts of terrorism that were committed primarily to gain headlines in the news media. He began to see that reporters could cause violence by reporting it and decided to use the cannibal as a metaphor for terrorists in the film he would make.

In the movie, Robert Kerman, who is better known in this country for his appearances in porno films as Richard Bolla, plays a reporter sent into the jungle to find out what happened to a team of reporters who had vanished there. He locates a tribe that has the footage the team shot. He manages to make a trade for it and then returns to civilization.

The footage tells what happened. The team was making a film of the tribe's most repugnant rituals, not unlike the "Mondo" movies that are so popular on video. The things that the tribe did became so repellent that the reporters decided to kill them. They did so in ways that were just as barbarous as what the tribe had done.

But they were going against an enemy they did not understand. Before long, the tribe would have them, and it would be the tribe's turn to torture, maim, and kill.

Shortly after it was released in Italy, all prints were confiscated by the police, and Deodato was hauled into court. He was charged with making an obscene film. The case dragged on for two years before Deodato was finally cleared.

During this time, he was unable to work. When the trouble was over, all that producers wanted from him was another cannibal film. *Cannibal Holocaust* was going through the roof. But he had done all he could in the genre. The two films were so intense that he did not think he could say any more. He has made several other movies since then, but none so visceral as his cannibal films.

Stephen C. Apostoloff: Better known as A. C. Stephen, the name he directed several softcore efforts under, Apostoloff was a prolific filmmaker in the late 1960s and early 1970s. Though no one would go so far as to say he was a talented director, he did the best he could on some of the lowest budget films in a genre that was known for tight-fisted productions.

His 1965 film *Orgy of the Dead* is perhaps the best known, primarily because of the involvement of Ed Wood and Wood-regular Criswell. Many people refer to this as Wood's movie, hardly even giving credit to Apostoloff. And it does resemble much of Wood's work. I suspect that Wood never had another director who would follow one of his scripts so closely. Apostoloff even had Wood's rotten luck with shooting day-for-night scenes. On the drive the couple takes before winding up in the graveyard, one shot looks like night, the next daytime, then back to night.

As was previously mentioned in this chapter, Criswell was the Devil, the couple were his captives, and the souls of the dead were some of the better strippers working in the mid–1960s. Apostoloff filmed it almost all on one set, keeping costs down. Since this was just a rather strange version of the 1950s striptease movies, there was no real reason to have more than one set.

Keeping sets to a minimum and shooting almost entirely indoors would come to be Apostoloff's trademarks. After he finished the striptease movie, he would join the ranks of softcore producers, where his shoot it fast and cheap style was necessary to compete.

He came up with a string of movies with the word *Confidential* in the title. Though *Confidential Magazine* had passed its peak back in the late

1950s, it tarred that word for many years to come. Anything with *confidential* in the title carried an aura of sleaze. It made Apostoloff's series a sure seller in the grindhouses that would play such fare.

There was *Suburbia Confidential* in 1966, *Motel Confidential* in 1967, and *College Girl Confidential* in 1968. The year 1968 was a busy one for him. In addition to the last *Confidential* film, he made *The Bachelor's Dream* and *Office Love-in*.

These films, cinematically speaking, were just a step above stag movies. They were done on simple sets and shot in such a way as to minimize changes in lighting, therefore saving time. There were two types of scenes in these films, dialogue scenes, and sex scenes. In the dialogue scenes, people sit and talk or stand and talk. About as active as they ever get is to take a drink. The sex scenes were carefully shot to abide by all the taboos of the softcore era.

The 1970s would see Apostoloff directing another Ed Wood script, *Fugitive Girls*. One of the girls was porno star Renée Bond. The sex films were creating their own "name" players by then. Among them was softcore star Marsha Jordan, who would act in the title role of Apostoloff's *The Divorcée*.

To this point, Apostoloff had used the name A. C. Stephen on all his work. But when he made the movie *Hot Ice*, he decided to put his own name in the credits. This film, about a man and woman con artist team who go into hiding at a ski lodge, was an attempt to find a different audience. The softcore market was fizzling out, quickly being replaced by hardcore films. Apostoloff wanted to make a cheap R-rated crime caper movie for the drive-ins. Unfortunately, his style of filmmaking hadn't changed a bit. The film just looked like a tamer version of one of his softcore films.

Index

Abel, Robert 29
The Adventures of Lucky Pierre 30, 45, 142, 158–160, 163, 170, 179
The Affair 75
Alex, Kirk 95, 97
Alex Joseph and His Wives 8
"Alfred Hitchcock Presents" 11
Ali, Muhammad 89
The Alien Dead 81
Allen, Jeffrey 35, 39, 169
Allen, Rusty 161, 162
The Amazing Transplant 147
"American Bandstand" 57
American Graffiti 176
Andersson, Harriet 155
Andy Warhol's Frankenstein 107
Another Day, Another Man 147
Ansara, Michael 8
Apostoloff, Stephen 176, 184, 185
Arnold, Mel 168
Arong, Domingo 86–89
Arong, Narcisco 86–89
Ashley, John 86
The Astro Zombies 1, 4, 8
Atrocities of War 119

Babb, Kroger 51–56, 115, 117, 151, 152, 154–156, 168
The Bachelor's Dream 185
Bad Girls Go to Hell 143, 145, 147
Baer, Max, Jr. 175, 176
Bagdad After Midnight 70
Balla, Richard 183
Balsam, Jerry 125, 126
Bauer, Michelle 83, 84
Baxter, Anne 157
Beatty, Warren 138

Beaudine, William 52, 129
Because of Eve 154, 156
Bell, Virginia 167, 168
Bell, Bare and Beautiful 167, 168, 180
Bell, Book, and Candle 72
Bellboy and the Playgirls 24
Beneath the Valley of the Ultravixens 50
Benny, Jack 94, 95
Bergman, Ingmar 56, 58, 155
"The Beverly Hillbillies" 175
Beyond the Valley of the Dolls 47
Bibo, Walter 25, 69
Biohazard 83
Black, Karen 25, 29, 157
The Black Klansman 4
Blacksnake 49–50
The Blast Off Girls 37
The Blob 23
Blood Feast 29, 30, 33, 34, 35, 45, 60, 68, 69, 100, 151, 161, 165, 168, 169, 170, 177, 179, 180
Blood Freak 177
Blood Orgy of the She Devils 6, 8
Blood Shack 22
Bloodthirsty Butchers 127
Bob and Sally 154
The Body Beneath 126
BOIN-N-G! 142, 145, 164, 180
Bond, Renee 185
Born Losers 38
Boulton, Lyn 168
Bowers, Bill 181
The Brain Leeches 80, 83
Brandt, Carolyn 16, 21
The Breast of Russ Meyer 50
Bride of the Monster 176
Browning, Tod 119

187

INDEX

Brownrigg, S. F. 134
Bruce, Lenny 70
Buchanan, Larry 129–138
"The Buddy Dean Show" 57, 66
Burns, Bob 105
Burns, Marilyn 105, 106, 109

Campos, Rafael 8
Cannibal 183
Cannibal Holocaust 182, 184
Carey, Timothy 12
Carnival Story 157
Carradine, John 1, 2
Carson, L. M. 103
Castle, William 57, 58, 65
"Charlie's Angels" 8
The Choppers 181
Chorus Call 173
City of Walking Dead 78
The Collector 172
College Girl Confidential 185
Color Me Blood Red 34, 35, 170, 179, 180
Coming in on the Wings of a Prayer 130
Concorde Affair 183
Coopman, John Pierre 89
Copenhagen's Psychic Loves 37, 70
Coppola, Carmen 23
Coppola, Francis Ford 23, 24
Corman, Roger 86, 102, 124
The Corpse Grinders 4–6, 7, 8
Cox and Underwood (agents) 51, 52
Crabbe, Buster 80, 81
The Crazies 76
Criswell 176, 184
Cry-Baby 66
Cukor, George 130
Curse of the Full Moon 127
Curse of the Queerwolf 93, 94, 95, 96

Dance Hall Racket 67, 70
Daughter of Horror 112, 177, 178
Daughter of the Son 161, 163, 170
Dawn of the Dead 71, 76, 77, 78
Deadly Weapons 146, 147, 149
Dean, James 42
Death Row Gameshow 93
DeCenzie, Pete 43

Deep Throat 107, 147
The Defilers 171, 172
The Degenerates 125
Dementia 13 23
Deodato, Ruggero 182, 183, 184
Depp, Johnny 66
The Depraved (Milligan) 125
The Depraved (Steckler-Haydock) 20
Desperate Living 64
Devil's Gambit 8
D'Hondt, Denica 29
Diary of a Nudist 142
Divine 58–63, 65
The Divorcée 185
The Doll Squad 8
Don't Look in the Basement 134
Double Agent 73, 145, 147, 149
Douglas, Kirk 2
Dowd, Tom 27, 39, 161, 163, 164
Down on Us 138
Downe, Allison Louise 37, 163, 165
Drive-in Sleaze (1934–70) 67
Drivers in Hell 12
Dunaway, Faye 138
Duras, Marguerite 65
Dust to Dust 51

Eat Your Makeup 58
Ebert, Roger 47
Eden, Jerry 35, 161, 168, 169
Eegah! 12, 181, 182
Eggshells 103, 104, 105, 183
Elam, Jack 56
Elliott, Leslie 126
Elysia 69
Erotica 45
Esper, Dwain 70, 111–119, 151, 177
Europe in the Raw 45
Evans, Roger 94, 95
Eve and the Handyman 45
Exploitation Trailers 67
Expostulations 72
The Eye Creatures 133, 134
An Eye for an Eye 180

Falbo, Billy 30
Fangoria 101
Farrell, Timothy 70
Fassbinder, Rainer Werner 58

INDEX

Faster, Pussycat! Kill! Kill! 46, 47, 58
Father Bingo 55
Father Knows Best 65
Female Trouble 62, 63
Flagg, Cash 12, 16
Forbidden Love 116, 119
Ford, Art 121
Fowles, John 172
Foy, Bryan 51, 69
Freaks 116, 119
Free, White and 21 132
Frenzy 12
Friedman, David F. 25, 30, 45, 55, 68, 69, 142, 147, 151,
Frost, Lee 172
Fugitive Girls 176, 185
Fulci, Lucia 76, 78

Gacy, John Wayne 63
Gamecock of St. Peter (Manak Ni San Pedro) 88–90
Gant, Marya 91
Garden of Eden 69, 139, 142, 161
Gates of Hell 78
Gavin, Erica 47
Gein, Ed 103
Gentry, Bobby 176
George, Christopher 78
The Ghostly Ones 125, 126
Giant 42
The Girl Can't Help It 26
The Girl from Sin 70
The Girl, the Body, and the Pill 37
Glen or Glenda 176
Glore, Charles 35
The Godfather 23, 24
Golden, Pappy 119, 151
Golden Age Olympics 80
Goldilocks and the Three Bares 164, 180
Goodbye, Norma Jean 135, 137, 138
The Gore Gore Girls 39, 40
Grease 66
The Greatest Show on Earth 153
Gross, Jerry 81
The Gunfighter 130
Guys and Dolls 42

Hag in a Black Leather Jacket 58
Hairspray 66

Hale, Alan 2
Halfway to Hell 56
Hall, Arch, Jr. 181, 182
Hall, Arch, Sr. 12, 20, 181, 182
Hall, Scott 52, 168
Hansen, Gunnar 84, 105, 106, 109
Hargitay, Mickey 27
Hawkes, Steve 177, 179
Haydock, Ron 20, 21, 22
Hearst, Patricia 66
Heavenly Bodies 45
Hefner, Hugh 43, 179
The Heisters 102
Hell Raiders 135
Hell's Angels 69, 100
Hemingway, Ernest 42
Hendrix, Jimi 138
Henkel, Kim 101, 103–105
High School Confidential 27
High School Girl 51
High Yellow 132
Hinton, Michael 89
History of the World, Part 1 84
Hitchcock, Alfred 11, 100, 109
Hollywood Chainsaw Hookers 83, 110
Hollywood Strangler Meets the Skid Row Slasher 21, 22
Holt, Tim 39
Hometown USA 176
Hooper, Tobe 99–110, 183
Horn, Marilyn 52
Hot Ice 185
How to Undress in Front of Your Husband 113
Howe, Anne 68
Hunt Brothers 85
Hunter, Tab 65
Hurkos, Peter 36
Hurley, James F. 36, 37

I Married a Savage 70
The Immoral Mr. Teas 30, 41, 44, 45, 60, 69, 142, 145
The Immoral West 45
Incredibly Strange Creatures Who Stopped Living and Became Mixed Up Zombies 14–18, 20, 21
Indian Fighter 2
Invasion of the Saucermen 133
It's Alive 135

Jackson, Eli 167, 180
Jada 131
Jailbait 176
Jessop, Robert 134
Jet Benny 94
Johnson, Tor 23
Joplin, Janis 138
Jordon, Marsha 185
Joseph, Irwin 154, 155, 157, 158, 161
Jungle Holocaust 173
Just for the Hell of It 39

Karimoja 56
Keep My Grave Open 134
Kennedy, John F. 131, 132
Kerman, Robert 183
Kerwin, Rooney, 181
Kerwin, William 29, 30, 34, 37, 168, 169, 179–181
Kestekian, Dennis 18
Keyholes Are for Peeping 147, 148
Kiel, Richard 12, 182
Kill the Dragon 8
King, Atlas 16, 17, 18
King, Claude 40
Kiss Me Deadly 165
Kohlberg, Stan 165, 168, 170
Kovacs, Laslo 17, 172

Lake, Rikki 66
Lancaster, Stuart 46
Landis, James 182
LaRose, Rose 30, 158
The Last Cannibal World 182
Last Feelings 183
The Last Survivor 183
The Last Time I Saw Archie 181
The Lawless Rider 176
Leeds, Lila 56
Levine, Joseph E. 139
Lewis, Floyd 154
Lewis, H. G. 25, 29–40, 45, 58, 59, 68, 75, 97, 100, 125, 142, 147, 151, 157–165, 167–170, 172, 177, 179–180, 181
Linda and Abilene 39
Live Like a Cop, Die Like a Man 183
Living Venus 29, 157, 158, 168, 179
Livingston, Shelby 169

Liz 122–124
LoBianco, Tony 147
Lochary, David 60
Lords, Traci 66
Loren, Sophia 24, 25
Lorna 34, 45, 46, 142, 143, 165
Love Me Tender 179
Lugosi, Bela 177
Lunchmeat 97

McCarty, John 105
Macon County Line 175
McQueen, Steve 23
Magic Spectacles 181
Maitland, Lorne 46
The Man from U.N.C.L.E. 70
Mandrake (the magician) 1
Maniac 70, 111, 112, 177
The Maniacs Are Loose 18
Manning, Marilyn 181
Mansfield, Jayne 25–27
March of Crime 113
Marihuana: Weed with Roots in Hell 67, 70, 111, 113
Marlowe, Rex 164
The Marrying Kind 130
Mars Needs Women 129, 134, 135
Martin 76
Marx, Harpo 12
Mason, Connie 168, 169
Massey, Edith 64
Matinee Idol 173
Medved Brothers 101, 176
Merriwether, Nicholas 182
Meyer, Russ 25, 30, 34, 41–50, 58, 69, 111, 143, 157
Micelli, Joe 17, 18
Mikels, Ted V. 1–10, 142
Milligan, Andy 73, 111, 121–128
Mishkin, William 123–127
Mr. Hulot's Holiday 44
Mitchum, Robert 56, 181
Modern Motherhood 115, 117
Moede, Titus 20, 21
Mom and Dad 52, 53, 55, 56, 115, 152, 154, 156, 168
Mondo Cane 59
Mondo Trasho 59, 60, 65
Monica: The Story of a Bad Girl 56, 155

Monroe, Marilyn 25, 26, 138
Monster a Go-Go! 36
Moonshine Mountain 35, 36
Morgan, Chesty 147, 149
Morgan, George T. 13, 20
Morgan, Georgia 9
Moro, Aldo 183
Morrison, Jim 138
Motel Confidential 185
Mudhoney 46
Multiple Maniacs 59, 60, 65

Naked Complex 145
The Naked Witch (Buchanan) 130
The Naked Witch (Milligan) 124, 125
Narcotic 113
Natividad, Kitten 83
Nature Girl 139, 147
Nature's Mistakes 116, 120
Nature's Playmates 163, 164
Naughty Dallas 131, 132
The Navy vs. the Night Monsters 27
Neal, Ed 104, 105, 107, 109
Night of the Living Dead 71, 72–75, 76
A Night to Dismember 149
Nightbirds 126
Niles, Fred 29
Noonan, Tommy 27
The Notorious Daughter of Fanny Hill 172
Nude on the Moon 142, 147

Obadiah 18 8
Ode to Billy Joe 176
Office Love-in 185
O'Hara, Bette 17
Olsen, Astrid 69
One Too Many 55
Operation Overkill 8
Orgy of the Dead 176, 184
Ornitz, Dan 42, 43
Oswald, Lee Harvey 131, 132, 135
The Ox-Bow Incident 130

Parker, John 177
Partain, Paul 105
Pasolini, Pier Paolo 58
Patton 42
Pearce, Mary Vivian 61

Pearl, Daniel 105
Peter, Paul & Mary 102
The Phantom Empire 84
Pin Down Girls 67
Pink Flamingoes 60, 61, 63, 64
Pirro, Mark 90–93
Plan 9 from Outer Space 112, 176, 177
Playgirl Killer 181
A Polish Vampire in Burbank 91, 92
Polyester 65, 66
Poor White Trash 2 134
Presley, Elvis 177, 179
The Prime Time 25, 29, 157, 158
The Prince of Peace 55
The Promiscuous Sex 124
Promises, Promises 25, 27
The Psychic 37, 70
Psycho 100

Rat Pfink a Boo Boo 11, 20, 21
The Rats Are Coming, the Werewolves Are Here 127
Ray, Fred Olen 79–84
Rebane, Bill 36
The Rebel Jesus 138
Reems, Harry 147
Renay, Liz 18
Revenge of the Ripper 22
Reynolds, Quentin 56
Ricci, Mark 73
Ricci, Rudy 71, 73
Roberts, Oral 130
Robot Monster 70
Rogers, Wayne 3
Romero, George 71–78
Rossellini, Roberto 183
Rowe, Misty 136
Ruby, Jack 131, 132
Russo, John 71, 73

Sack, Al 158
The Sadist 182
Sager, Ray 37
Santamaria, Erick 181
Satana, Tura 2, 8, 41, 46, 58
Savini, Tom 76
Scalps 81–83
Schmidt, Wolfgang 21, 22
Scott, Chuck 35

INDEX

Scum of the Earth 31, 32, 34, 45, 142, 154, 165, 166, 167, 180
"Sea Hunt" 88
Season of the Witch 75–76
The Secrets of Beauty 55
Sellers, Peter 72
Seven into Snowy 173
The Seven Minutes 49
Severinson, Doc 147
Sex Maniac 113
The Sex Perils of Paulette 147
She Devils on Wheels 37, 100
She Shoulda Said No 56
Shock Value 47, 58
Sholem, Lee 129
Siedow, Jim 104, 106, 107, 109
Silverman, Louis 147
Sinclair, Sandy 167
Singin' in the Sun 164
Siskel and Ebert 82–83
Sleazemania 67
A Smell of Honey, a Swallow of Brine! 172
The Smut Peddler 68, 69
Something Weird 36, 37
Sommaren Med Monica 155
Sonney, Dan 170
Sonney, Louis 112, 113
Sonney family 151, 157
Sorg, Adam 35, 170
The Sound of Music 90
Space Angels 8
Spillane, Mickey 165
Splatter 109
Splatter Movies 105
Star Wars 94
Starlet 172
Starr, Blaze 141, 143, 147
Steckler, Ray Dennis 11–22, 182
Stephen, A. C. 176, 184, 185
Stole, Mink 60, 66
Storm, Tempest 43
Strange Rampage 68, 69
Strawberries Need Rain 135
Street Corner 154
Streiner, Russell 71, 73
Strike Me Deadly 3, 4, 8
Suburban Roulette 37, 181
Suburbia Confidential 185
Superchick 38
Supervixens 50

Susann, Jacqueline 48
Sweetwood, Thomas 30, 34, 180

The Taking of Pelham One Two Three 107, 108
Talbot, Lyle 56
Talley, Gidney 154
Tamblyn, Russ 27
A Taste of Blood 37, 181
Tate, Sharon 60
Teas, Bill 42, 44
Teenage Psycho Meets Bloody Mary 15
Ten Violent Women 8, 9, 10
Terror at Halfday 36
The Texas Chainsaw Massacre 97, 99–102, 103, 104–109, 183
The Texas Chainsaw Massacre, Part Two 103, 109
This Stuff'll Kill Ya 39
Thompson, William C. 112, 177, 178
Three Nuts in Search of a Bolt 27
The Thrill Killers 18–19, 20, 21,
Tijuana After Midnight 70
The Tingler 57
Tom Jones 45
The Tomb 83, 84
Tonight for Sure 23, 24
Torso 100
The Trial of Lee Harvey Oswald 135
Tucker, Phil 70
Two Nights with Cleopatra 24, 25
Two Thousand Maniacs 30, 34, 35, 60, 97, 169, 170, 179, 180

The Undertaker and His Pals 6, 7
Up! 50

The Valley of the Dolls 47, 49, 172
Van Doren, Mamie 27
Vigeant, Phil 97
Violence in America 101
The Violent Years 176
Vixen 47

Wallace, Irving 49
Ware, Bunny 68

Warhol, Andy 47
Waters, John 47, 57–66, 111
Watters, William, 182
Weirdo 128
Weisenborn, Gordon 29
West, Mae 26
What's Up Front 181
Whitman, Dawn 147
Wild Guitar 11, 12–13, 16, 182
The Wild, Wild World of Jayne Mansfield 27
Wilkinson, June 24
Willard 127
The Windsplitter 104
Winters, Shelley 139
Wisher, Doris 147
Wishman, Doris 139–149
The Wizard of Gore 37
Wood, Ed 70, 111, 176, 177, 184, 185

Wood, Thomas 30, 180
The World of Sleaze 67
The World's Greatest Sinner 12

Yang, Tiger 8
Yeager, Bunny 161
Year of the Yahoo 40
York, Francine 8
Young, Ralph 147
Youngman, Henny 39
A Youth in Babylon 172

Zombie 76–78
Zombie Flesh Eaters 78
Zombie II 78
Zontar: The Thing from Venus 129
Zorita 70
Zsigmond, Vilmos 17

www.ingramcontent.com/pod-product-compliance
Ingram Content Group UK Ltd.
Pitfield, Milton Keynes, MK11 3LW, UK
UKHW042006140426
5217IPUK00015B/1022